Buy that Business...

Poor old Daddy didn't leave you!

Richard C. Shumaker

ISBN-10: 1515064247
ISBN-13: 978-1515064244

DEDICATION

To the management team, long on experience, but short on cash; to the small business person, full of ambition, but short on the knowledge associated with mergers and acquisitions; to the bright, struggling entrepreneur who just once wants to get hold of a successful business; to the business broker who cannot finance an otherwise qualified client; and, of course, to many other individuals and groups: particular minorities; the handicapped, often the underdog; seniors citizens who still have all their talents, but lack an opportunity; small well-meaning churches and towns; various non-profit organizations with more heart than money; to each of you, I dedicate this writing with the genuine hope that readers shall choose to seek benefit from its teachings...*Richard C. Shumaker*

Buy That Business ... Poor old Daddy didn't Leave you!

A Disclaimer

The Copyright Notice

Buy That Business ... Poor old Daddy didn't Leave you!

CONTENTS

Buy That Business ... Poor old Daddy didn't Leave you!

INTRODUCTION

Most people who seek me are deficient in funding and credit, but have the desire and experience to acquire and operate a company. Management teams, owners desiring to expand operations and ambitious entrepreneurs who do not what to start a business from scratch are examples of clients. My methods are known to often eliminate or replace the need for traditional banking methodologies, are unique in nature, and for the most part, are easy to implement once understood.

Over the years I have assembled some of the most dramatic, yet simplistic, business acquisition packages ever devised by a business consultant. Some are successful, some are not, but that is the nature of the business world.

Because of my innate shyness and inability to sell anything to anyone, I have always had to develop techniques that work regardless of my ineffectual being. So I create techniques that sometimes work too well, or sound too good. Because of that, my procedures have often been misinterpreted, misunderstood, or misused. Consequently, even though my methods are perfected, protected and practicable, I have been both acclaimed and ridiculed, dubbed everything from a business person to be afraid of to a financial genius. Readers will have to form their own opinion.

My processes leverage natural assets usually overlooked within the business environment. The process has become known as the Natural Business Philosophy. Its teachings are logical, practical and extremely effective and frugal.

Besides financial purchasing power through leverage, various methods described are generally aimed at realistically reducing debt service.

After all, even if the decision is made to buy a company, what are the odds that success will be lasting if debt service is enormous and out of line with generally accepted accounting ratios?

Existing businesses with debt can likewise profit by the techniques explained here. Whether debt exists, or will be part of the closing, the goals are always to eventually eliminate the liability.

Nevertheless, more profound and more significant than my ability to put together business packages, there has been a recent underlying conviction that there is more to life than mere goal achievement.

Now, the philosophy lesson:

All my life I chased goals, but recently came to the judgment that goal chasing - the secret to success many say - is superficial and takes one's attention away from living. Once a goal is achieved, it is no longer fulfilling. Whereas before, I toiled deliberately, fumed on every front, and when faced with a lack of fulfillment, shook my head a lot. What I do now is create, write and educate; thus, the reason for this manuscript.

For me, goal setting has given way to purpose; outside motivation has been replaced by internal exhilaration; and, always living for tomorrow is no longer. The journey along the way is pure enjoyment. I found out what really makes me happy. Since I adopted this conviction, my personal existence has taken on new meaning. Life is more interesting, more fulfilling and more productive. Things happen more naturally, most often without tension.

Here is my hope for readers:

Perhaps this writing inspires readers - some anyway - to reach for milestones thought impossible, yet enjoy the trip. In other words, go after what you want, but find pleasure during the journey. Perhaps a few readers will even find individual purpose, but that is an intangible objective.

To follow that notion, if asked what our purpose here is on earth, many might say that the answer has something to do with religion, or God. Others think that there is no explanation at all. We are here simply because generation after generation has bred. Yet, should there in fact be a reason for our residency here, maybe it has to do with contribution. After all, history remembers those who contribute to society, move people, or change the course of events. Regardless, most of us will never meet that standard. Most of us will live and die without so much as a mention in any book, let alone remembered by historians.

A life lived simply until death without contributing something to humanity is without meaning!

To reach a point whereby contribution is possible, the lack of money and self-doubt must first be overcome. Money always seems to be a fundamental deficiency and self-doubt is frequently the result from years of disappointment and criticism.

The older we get, the wiser we get; the wiser we get, the dumber we get; the dumber we get, the more frightened we get. Fear dissipates dreams.

End of the philosophy lesson.

Bottom line: There is a way to defeat what may seem to be a formidable task, to overcome money shortages and self-doubt regardless of the environment conditions. The answer is not an easy one; the path is strewn with hard work and cumbersome detail. Yet, the course is straight and narrow. Results are predictable and only contingent on understanding the guidelines and putting forth appropriate effort. For those ready to challenge what appears to be an impossible dream, to march into an unfamiliar realm, to risk censure - grab the power.

When faced with one of life's rivers, too wide and too deep to cross, first, swim half way. If you must row, sink the boat when you get to the middle.

Go into the business community and buy a business!

Yes, buy a business even with meager capital and limited credit. Buy a vigorous business, and with diligent application. Readers will be shown how to do it, where to look, what to look for and how to get the money. In fact, users will be able to act as if they are a financial institution. There is no guarantee of success, but chance for acquisition success is dramatically boosted.

The program is not a get-rich-quick scheme and certainly not like playing the lotto. Practitioners will have to work and work hard, be willing to take definite chances and be able to soak up more about cash and cash flow than many bankers do. Whether with purpose or mere goal setting, whatever the reason to acquire a business, the wherewithal can be found in and among the lines of scrawl that follow.

So, to all timid souls absorbed in self-doubt, who hunger for an enduring monument, arise and conquer! The time is now and the path has been cut. Stand up and get moving.

Forget about security blankets. Security is one basis for mediocrity and boredom!

The following chapters may be the most exciting reading ever, or the most irksome. So what are you waiting for? Get started!

...*Richard C. Shumaker, author*

Chapter One: The Natural Business Philosophy

Prologue

The Natural Business Philosophy is a reasoned doctrine conceived to expose unique financial enhancement tools found in most small business, but ordinarily ignored by owners and management. Once uncovered and used, these tools give the operator access to strong monetary means. The philosophy is simple, yet powerful, and the more fully it is understood, the greater its usefulness.

Anyone who has climbed an apple tree knows that the juiciest fruits are found most distant from the trunk, farthest out on the limb, where branches grow narrow and hard to sit. All the red beauties are out there, daring to be picked. Venture too close and risk a fall. Shake the branches and many drop, but seldom will the ones most sought. Left unpicked, all the apples will end on the ground to rot. What to do?

Get a ladder! Find one with hefty footing and thick rungs, yet, lightweight. That way, anyone can cart it from point to point. Make sure the ladder can support a lot of weight and when set in place, it stays put. Climb the ladder, not the tree. Snap off only the pick of the crop. No longer risk falling.

To understand how a ladder makes picking apples more efficient and less hazardous helps to illustrate how some business owners, using resourceful financial technology (a ladder), might achieve - heretofore missed - advantageous corporate opportunities (a red, juicy apple). This technological know-how is called the Natural Business Philosophy. Cash management makes it work. Its yield absolutely overwhelms the average business person's mind.

Just like the ladder, resourceful cash management supports a lot of weight, financial weight that is, and when set in place, stays put. It's lightweight, too. Once comprehended, these procedures meet most financial challenges.

Re-Introduction to a Vintage Business Principle

Perceived as the inventive utilization of inherent corporate strengths to improve productivity and operational stability, the Natural Business Philosophy promotes greater productivity, greater business profits and increased overall financial stability.

Doubtless George Westinghouse - the man given credit for creating the giant railroad and natural gas industries as well as beginning the Age of Electricity - was far ahead of his time. Known as possibly the most prolific inventor of all time, this talented genius also provided us with one first glimpse into what doing business the natural way meant.

Westinghouse Enters the Natural Business Arena

In 1881, Westinghouse established the first one-half day off for his employees: Saturday. What did that accomplish? Greater production and loyalty from employees. From within the bounds of his corporate environment, Westinghouse saw a natural way to increase his company's productivity; thus more profit and greater financial stability.

In 1908, he established a pension fund. In 1913, Westinghouse offered paid vacations. The result? Employee loyalty. Loyalty led to retention of skilled labor, better products, better service and a more solid business reputation.

Electronic Finance

Doing business the natural way represents years of solid small business experience - success-oriented ventures and those that failed - plus the learned insight to avoid the latter. This philosophy knows how small

14

businesses think, what small businesses need and how to grow small businesses. The philosophy is a problem solver: Describe the guidelines; it acts, searches for opportunities, analyzes findings and helps bring about win-win terms and conditions. There has never been a process easier to perform or simpler to understand.

Once the natural business approach is altogether comprehended, small business practitioners quickly learn that implementation of its principles may usher forth remarkable operational improvement in areas of finance and equity.

Financial enhancement comes as less debt service - long term or short - and increased cash and cash equivalent numbers. Equity enhancement results from greater cash reserves and less debt service, or higher revenues with less overhead expenses.

Comparison to Homeopathic Medicine

Similar to Homeopathic medicine - belief in the natural healing of the body - the Natural Business Philosophy advocates operating small business within the realm of what is natural, intuitive and practicable.

Some say that taking an aspirin for a headache may stop the ache, but neglects to solve the problem causing the headache. If the reason for a headache is dehydration, taking an aspirin only solves the symptom. Take a glass of water in lieu of the tablet and the root issue is resolved - only in a natural way.

If a small business operates outside the realm of what is natural, money (an aspirin by analogy), when embraced as the all-encompassing solution to heal any financial problem (a headache by analogy), might temporarily solve any difficulty, but the root issue that caused the monetary problem (dehydration by comparison) may remain.

Solve the Problem First

Solve the reason for a financial problem first, then there might be less need to borrow money. Unfortunately, most small business people tend to think that money solves all financial matters regardless of the root of the difficulty. Nevertheless, less borrowing clearly means less debt service and less debt generally promotes both a stronger growth and a more stable fiscal condition within any business entity.

Program Objectives

No longer is it possible for business to think of employees first. Government regulations and union authority now demand greater attention. Banks determine who receives a loan, no longer based on natural merit or community benefit, but profit. In public companies, stockholder interests give way to management teams who struggle to hold position and power.

Small business is left out in the cold when it comes to competing on what has become a playground for big business and government. Forget the fact that most small businesses fail, or that banks only give loans to those with healthy financial statements. Small business has little chance to compete, grow and succeed.

New Hope

To offer new hope to the small business owner who strives to compete, grow and succeed, this program takes a turn back to the days when a more natural, more honest approach survived. Not that all things were perfect, but for the small business owner, success came to those who most successfully paid their bills, found ways to expand operations and kept best track of operations.

Natural methodology, once exposed, teaches small business entrepreneurs how to increase effectively liquidity, expand operations and control expenses. However, the philosophy presumes that the practitioner is versed in good solid business basics. Without fundamentals in business practices, it would be virtually impossible for readers to apply what is learned here.

Buy That Business ... Poor old Daddy didn't Leave you!

Chapter Two: The Theory of Theories

There is no way under the sun that any reader will be able to fully comprehend and then implement any financial process hereinafter described without first grasping the theory behind each procedure. The rationale behind each financial technique is absolutely indispensable to the successful application of the process. Without this insight, when faced with an information base that fails to meet exactly what has been resolved to be the most appropriate criterion to success, the reader/user will surely pass up potential, profitable opportunities.

During the examination of innumerable acquisitions possibilities over the years, from each batch of about 20, two generally jumped out as good candidates. However, on closer examination, because of my intimate understanding of the theories behind the financing procedures, I am usually able to qualify closer to six from each group.

Pick a Winner

A buyer's ability to perform financially is the first priority when it comes to the selection of a potential candidate for acquisition. From any list of businesses for sale, the ones that are most likely to fit the criteria set by the Natural Business Philosophy are chosen. Which one do you want to pursue is the question? This is pure entrepreneurial endeavor, logical and most frugal. However, the process is in direct conflict with what is considered normal acquisition seeking methodology.

Usually a business person who desires to expand will establish guidelines that fit a particular need. For example, say a certain business manufactures computers. The owner may logically determine that for another company to qualify for purchase, the company must be able to meet certain standards: Revenues over $10,000,000; adjusted earnings greater than 10%; assets in excess of $2,000,000; an ability to produce similar computer components; a non-union work force; and, so on. But, in the end, to find such a business might prove unrealistic; it may not exist; the cost to purchase may prove beyond ability to perform; and, the time necessary to find such a business might be out of proportion to the effort. The NBP does not work this way.

To acquire a company by using the techniques found in the Natural Business Philosophy and succeed where many others fail, requires users to look beyond words. Get at the theory!

The Theory

Understanding the hypothesis associated with any process is almost as important as the process itself. Take friction for example. George Westinghouse understood the meaning of friction, as do most people. Friction has to do with resistance; it causes objects to slow down. Simple enough. The average person encounters friction every day and is very familiar with it and what it means. Still and all, Westinghouse took this understanding and applied it to making railroad trains run more efficiently, or I should say start and stop more efficiently.

Until the time of George Westinghouse, large springs were mounted on the coupler assembly of each train to absorb the forces from sudden stopping and starting. Trains would often break in two from such force. Thus, 30 cars was the average maximum load that a single engine could handle.

Westinghouse invented a friction draft gear - called by some more important even than his famous air brake - which absorbed and dissipated energy by the rubbing of metal wedges against metal surfaces inside the coupler assembly. The result was a smoother operation when it came to stopping and starting. Consequently, many more cars could be added to a train.

George not only understood the theory associated with friction, but he applied his understanding to an invention that helped modernize railroading; theory before application.

Another example of theory before application is sterilization. Not until the Civil War did we understand that to sterilize medical instruments and hospital environments decreased infection, sickness and death. When fastidious nurses, caring for wounded soldiers at one particular hospital began keeping the premises clean and sterile, it became noticeably evident that fewer patients died and more got better sooner. Today, we take sterilization for granted.

Once it was understood that sterilizing medical equipment not only reduced the occurrences of death, but also hastened healing, the entire medical profession adopted the practice. Theory, then application.

Henry Ford developed through observation his theory of mass production. As simple as the theory was to anyone who heard about it, until Henry applied what he had learned, it was merely just one more premise. Anyone can profess understanding once given the thought, but Ford, as did Westinghouse, not only understood a specific theory, but also advanced it.

As with Westinghouse and Ford, there is a need for each reader to grasp the theory behind each of the processes presented in this writing before attempting application. Without understanding the thought behind the application, there will be little chance to broaden the usage when confronted with data not absolutely fitted to a particular event.

Losers

One more point while in this chapter: Do not go after losers! From experience, a company that is in financial difficulty today will probably be in financial difficulty tomorrow. I have been there! No matter how tempting it may be to find and easily close such a business, do not! Look for the best businesses on the market. Pass on any that are in financial difficulty. The Natural Business Philosophy provides sufficient capital resources to accomplish solid acquisitions.

Again: Do not go after losers!

Chapter Three: Where to Start

Find the Right Company

To best benefit from the methodology connected with the Natural Business Philosophy, locate only companies that can be leveraged using the philosophy processes. For example, companies with liens against receivables are usually not strong candidates for the NBP. Accounts receivable (money owed the company) represent one of the most important assets because they can be leveraged easily and quickly. If receivables are liened, leverage is impossible. To purchase a business without sufficient leverage is difficult. However, liens against other assets, such as equipment, real estate and inventory are less liable to strike a candidate from consideration.

For purposes to better understand specifically what companies qualify for acquisition under the NBP, here are some general guidelines to follow. To more fully comprehend the approach, reread this section after investigating the balance of this writing. To reread the material over and over will produce immense dividends.

Why is the Business for Sale?

The first question that must be asked the seller is "Why is the business for sale?" Many owners do not tell the real reason for disposal. Maybe to tell the truth makes the business less desirable. To compensate for this dilemma, always make the presumption that the business is in financial difficulty. Compel the seller to prove otherwise.

Perhaps in lieu of financial problems there is a creditable motivation to sell the business. Sickness, retirement or other interests are examples. Investigate any answer that does not make sense. If the business proves profitable, why does the seller want to dispose of long-term income? Is the owner really sick? Is the seller too young to retire?

Does the operator really have other interests? Good questions. Ask them.

Here are more questions to ask: Why has the owner not first looked to sell to management, a family tie, or a long-time employee? If the business is listed with a business broker, why? Many entities are sold locally or, to competition. Ads are run in pertinent magazines, newspapers, or on the Internet. Have ads been run? How long has the business been on the market? What does the competition, neighborhood gossip and management have to say about the pending sale? Hit the employees too - tactfully. These and other questions need to be asked. They are good questions and deserve worthy answers. Without a reliable answer for these questions, it is difficult to determine why the business is for sale.

Without knowing why the business is for sale, a buyer may try to construct a hopeful future on top of an unreliable past. No amount of due diligence (in depth operational study) can replace the need to discover why the business is for sale - the real reason.

What is the real reason that the business is for sale?

Minimum five Years in Operation

Businesses that fail generally fail during the first five years of operation. Some statistics say that as many as eight out of ten businesses crash within the first five years of existence. Consequently, a sensible buyer should not consider any business as a candidate for acquisition that has not been in business for at least five years. Although five years does not guarantee that the business will be successful for another five years, the fact that the operation has survived that long gives a potential buyer a semblance of constancy.

Only consider businesses for sale that have been in operation for five years or longer.

Management in Place

The big question here is this: What happens if you wake up some morning and the business you never got from dear old dad is suddenly yours? You really found, negotiated, financed and closed on a million-dollar business! You are the one who is in charge! Your dream has come true! Now what?

If you are relatively unseasoned in the business world, your dream will soon become a nightmare if you do not have a good team of competent management personnel in place. An owner-operated management staff of one simply does not cut it.

When the owner alone runs the business, there is only one boss, one operator and one person at the top. Why is that bad? Simple. When the boss leaves, who will run the company? Also, it means that if the boss were to leave, even for a short time, the operation may suffer greatly.

Another reason to be leery of one-person operations has to do with business relationships. Contacts, business wherewithal and employee allegiance often hinge on the owner. Without the owner's presence, there may in fact be no business. Beware of a business that is run by a sole proprietor who has not taken the time to build a management team - regardless of the reason.

Some owners are reluctant to give employees any information about the business or hand over authority to act on major issues. There is fear that maybe these same employees will go out on their own and start a competitive business. Owners are sometimes so arrogant that they will not share with others what they know, lest others will become as knowledgeable. Once uncovered, what mystery is left? The employees might lose respect. An owner who wants all the power all the time is obviously not interested in empowering a management group.

On the other hand, when an operation is too small to support a management agenda, there is perhaps an excuse for not having a team.

Regardless, do not assume that once in charge of a small business, a new owner is easily going to replace an owner who not only started the business, but after years of operation may be the only one who can run the business for profit.

When faced with a company too small to support a management team, the prudent action may be to pass up the opportunity.

Revenue on the Upswing

Operations that exhibit decreasing revenue over the past three years are obviously going in the wrong direction. Even if the loss of revenues can be explained due to a tightening of sales - sell less for more profit - there is still a lingering doubt as to why. Why after years of selling the same product or service does a company begin to lose revenues? In isolated instances there may be good cause, but usually it is best for a potential buyer to take the conservative approach to revenues loses.

Consider only potential candidates with either static revenues or revenues on the upswing over the past three years.

Satisfactory Corporate Credit

To perform several of the processes inherent to the Natural Business Philosophy, it is necessary to find companies with satisfactory credit. By no means is a triple-A rating required, but the operation must be able to substantiate that it can gain credit through the proper presentation of a corporate credit application. When asking for any kind of credit arrangement, the corporation must be the only one required to sign. An officer usually signs for the company, but not personally. Avoid personal signatures whenever possible. If not the case, certain of the methods described here will not function.

For the complete application of the philosophy, it is best to consider only business candidates with adequate credit.

Negotiable, Motivated Seller

A cooperative motivated seller is a must. If the owner is simply testing the waters to see what the company brings on the market, pass up the opportunity. If the seller is uncooperative in areas of seller financing, financial information, or critical points of negotiations, pass over the candidate. To find a seller who will openly and honestly negotiate with a buyer and who is highly motivated to sell, are two vital points essential to a successful purchase. Neither element is difficult to locate; most sellers are motivated. A motivated seller is one who will negotiate. Just make sure that the motivation to sell makes sense. Simply To dump a failing operation on the market is not a motivation that makes sense to a cautious buyer.

Cooperation is necessary. A seller must be ready and willing to lease out owned real estate especially if the buyer is unable or unwilling to purchase company real estate. The same goes for any equipment that is liened by a lender. Without this cooperation the buyer has little choice but to purchase the real estate or equipment. Sometimes that is financially impossible.

Get serious only with motivated, cooperative sellers.

Synergy

Synergy is a crucial part of business survival. It is "Connected activity." Synergy is more vital to business survival and business management than just about any other aspect of the corporate environment. Synergy is the connected action of all corporate components working together more efficiently than the total of each separate element running alone. It is most certainly crucial to corporate success.

Human employees interact with machines to decide, resolve and manage relevant issues. No business can survive let alone grow without this intercommunication. The employees identify specific uncertainties and devise plans and procedures that might help resolve the problems. They then count on machines to generate useful information about the problems and with speed beyond that which humans are capable, implement the plans and procedures.

The same applies between one employee and another. Successful cohesion between one employee and another, and employees and machinery, renders a more effective business operation.

There is no substitute for synergy and when a potential buyer of a business notices the absence of communication and accord, that buyer is better served to strike that business from consideration.

Chapter Four: How Much Should You Pay?

What is a company worth? The following discussion highlights several important elements applicable to price computation. Evaluation of an operation's worth is a complex assignment. After all, an owner is often selling something akin to a child. Years of drudgery, anxiety and heartache have gone into its upbringing and training. To figure how much the business is worth is downright complex.

Appraisals

Purchase price determination is subjective. Ask a business owner what his or her company is worth and chances are good that the answer will be far removed from a realistic appraisal. Likewise, request an appraisal of value from a business broker, and dependent on what software is loaded in the computer, value will vary all over the board. Since a broker's paycheck depends on selling listed businesses, what are the odds - in a competitive world - that an appraisal will be overblown just to sign the seller to a listing agreement? A buyer faces unrealistic expectations both ways.

Whether the value is placed by the seller, or by an agent of the seller, appraisals are inexact and the price set is often proportionate to the motivation of the one who makes the evaluation.

EBITDA

What then is a frugal buyer supposed to do?

A good rule of thumb is to price a business as a multiple of its earnings. Earnings are usually depicted as earnings before interest, taxes, depreciation and amortization (EBITDA). Earnings stated in this manner may also include owner benefits - wages, automobile expenses, insurance and so on paid by the corporation. These earnings are termed adjusted.

Make sure that expenses associated with replacing the owner are subtracted from earnings. Occasionally an owner, or the owner's agent, fails to consider what it will cost to replace the owner. Without that number subtracted from earnings, adjusted EBITDA is much too high. Any calculation of a purchase price based on this number is out of proportion with what is thought to be fair market value. Not only will the business not sell, but the buyer will be unable to leverage debt. A sharp buyer will already have dissected financial materials and conceived approximate estimates of valuation before discussing the purchase price for the company.

As to EBITDA, consider this: Depreciation, taxes and amortization are acceptable items to add back into the earnings equation, but when interest is added, watch what happens. If the corporation is in debt - say the receivables are liened by the local bank - the interest continues to be an ongoing debt service. What appear to be net earnings are only deemed real earnings if the company is debt free.

Often a business broker assesses the value of a company as if it is going to a buyer debt free. The buyer is not going to give the seller 100% cash so that all debt is paid off at closing. That is unrealistic. Normally the buyer takes over some or all the debt - payables, leases, etc.
A good rule of thumb is to price a business as a multiple of its earnings.

Times Four

To determine a fair selling price for corporate worth, stick close to a multiple times adjusted earnings no greater than four and a stockholder equity that can be leveraged sufficiently to purchase the operation. In some instances the multiple will be less and less is good. To purchase a company for three times adjusted earnings or less should be the initial goal of any careful buyer. A public company might sell its stock for as much as ten times earnings or more, especially after the initial offering. The major stock exchanges are overvalued such that certain market watchers say collapse is imminent.

To determine a fair selling price for corporate worth, stick close to a multiple times adjusted earnings no greater than four and a stockholder equity that can be leveraged sufficiently to purchase the operation.

Stockholder Equity

Another issue relative to purchase price is stockholder equity. Equity - in simplistic terminology - is the difference between what is owed by the corporation (liabilities) and what items of value it possesses (assets). Subtract liabilities from assets and stockholder equity is the result. If the corporation owes more than its assets, the company has a negative stockholder equity. When that occurs, the corporation is said to be technically bankrupt.

Some public companies are technically bankrupt, but their stock continues to trade because their earnings are high. Small private business corporations are usually not perceived that way. A small business with negative equity is viewed as a company in trouble.

Make certain that an acquisition candidate has a positive stockholder equity and that the multiple used to assess the value of the candidate comes close to the equity. In other words, if the company has an agreed on EBITDA of $250,000 and the purchase price negotiated is $1,000,000, make sure that the stockholders equity is not significantly under $1,000,000. Otherwise, to effect a suitable leveraged purchase of the company might be very difficult. Since, the equity of a company is the net result brought on by a comparison of assets and liabilities, when the purchase price is significantly greater than the net equity, where is the leverage potential? What is considered significant varies in each instance. If the receivables are not liened and the payables are equal to the receivables, the equity may be less than the purchase price. However, it does not matter as the receivables are sufficient to leverage the price.

Make certain that any acquisition candidate has a positive stockholders equity and that the multiple used to assess the value of the candidate comes close to the equity.

Break Even Financial Statements

Another rule of thumb is to consider only acquisition candidates that tender at least a break-even financial condition before recasting. Recasting is a term used by business brokers to adjust the earnings to what they consider more realistic. In most instances, a recast financial statement will bring earnings upward, but be troubled when recasting is necessary to bring the equity up passed zero. Usually this shows that the company is short on working capital.

Consider only acquisition candidates who tender at least a break-even financial condition before recasting.

Working Capital

Working capital is the difference between current liabilities and current assets. Current liabilities are debt such as payables - invoices the corporation owes another. Current assets are generally defined as cash on hand, receivables and inventory. Long term debt and certain assets - equipment and improvements to property - are not part of either current assets or current debt.

When the equity of a company is negative - liabilities are greater than assets - there is a good chance that working capital is negative, too. Negative working capital says that the company may not be able to pay debt service and may be in for a short-term existence. Important to remember: The NBP works best when exercised with good old-fashioned common sense!

Avoid candidates with negative working capital and negative stockholders equity.

Buy That Business ... Poor old Daddy didn't Leave you!

Chapter Five: The Math in Review

When a typical acquisition candidate is located and preliminary due diligence begins, a careful buyer will first make sure that the math works.

Adjusted Earnings

Does the seller accurately represent the earnings detail? Do the adjustments made to the earnings depict a precise account of financial consequences post-closing? Normal adjustments add back into corporate earnings the seller benefits that will no longer be withdrawn from expenses. Wages will be reduced, bonuses eliminated, vehicle benefits modified and so on. Any of these savings are true earnings because each will no longer occur post-closing.

Do each of the additions to earnings reflect the actual state of financial affairs after a buyer takes over the operation? To miscalculate expected profits is cataclysmic. Forget potential personal gain. Less earnings than planned make it impossible to pay debt service and taxes. There is nothing that occurs in the operation of a business that wreaks more havoc and produces more sleepless nights than to be powerless to pay debts and taxes.

Before a formal due diligence process, a buyer must have a comfort level as to the accuracy of the adjusted earning potential of the corporation. To think that they can be adjusted immediately after closing is just plain foolhardy. Earnings can be increased, but it takes time.

Adjusted earnings should be at least 3% to 5% X revenues. $12,000,000 yearly revenue should produce adjusted earnings of somewhere between $360,000 and $600,000, or more. Revised net dollars are earnings before taxes, interest, depreciation, amortization and owner benefits. Some companies earn more than 5%, others earn less. The type of company and the effectiveness of management help establish the earnings. The NBP works better if the earnings fall at 5%, a little above or, a little below.

A buyer must have a comfort level as to the accuracy of the adjusted earning potential of the corporation.

Suggested Revenue Requirements

There are many companies on the market with adjusted earnings above the 5% level. Most of those operations have revenues below NBP standards. A general rule, certainly with exceptions, is to seek larger revenue operations. The Natural Business Philosophy works best for companies with annual revenues over $12,000,000. That is not to say that the technology will not work with less income; it will, but to fall below annual income of less than $500,000 per month makes the task more complex.

Smaller businesses are more likely to have single-phase management, i.e., an individual owner in charge. The larger the company, the more likely that a management team is in place. More management usually equates to higher revenues. Since management costs money to put in place, profits are reduced - at least percentage-wise.

A company doing $12,000,000 with 5% earnings and a management team in place, produces the same dollars as a company with earnings of 25% against $2,400,000 income. The difference is probably due to management expenses. The former company might have six to eight management personnel; the latter has only one. So what is the incentive to grow a company? A single person makes as much money as a team. Not really.

There are problems on both sides of the fence - a single manager operation versus a management team organization. A management team generally is more successful in maintaining profits, staying in business longer and growing. There are more heads, more ideas, more creative juices and more experience. In the long run, there are also more dollars made.

The mathematics of the NBP partially relies on how the revenue stream compares to assets and selling price. Selling prices most often depend on adjusted income. When the calculations show that the revenue stream is out of proportion to profits, the process is more convoluted. To keep matters efficient, seek companies with adjusted earnings times a negotiated multiple no greater than 20% times the annual revenue stream; 25% tops. To do this requires considering companies whose revenues are at least $500,000 per month; better to consider operations with a minimum intake of $1,000,000 per month.

There are plenty of available business opportunities on the market from which to choose, but it takes time and patience to sort through the listings. Practitioners of the Natural Business Philosophy may even find a company or two in the public sector.

In the world of public companies, there are normally several listed entities on the three major stock exchanges whose market value (number of shares of stock outstanding multiplied by the current price per share) falls well within the bounds of what the Natural Business Philosophy might finance. Think you can run a public company?

The Natural Business Philosophy works best for companies with annual revenues over $12,000,000. Less revenue stream will of course often work, but the task is more difficult.

Selling Price Calculation

Expressed previously, one way to calculate the selling price of a business is to multiply the adjusted earnings times three; four maximum. A $12,000,000 revenue producing operation with adjusted earnings of $360,000 might have a suggested selling price of between $1,080,000 and $1,440,000. At $600,000 the range is $1,800,000 to $2,400,000. If a business broker is involved in the transaction, the upper end of the scale is usually asked. When an owner appraises the business, there is no telling what the price will be. One thing is for sure: An appraisal by the business owner, especially if the owner is the founder, will be higher than what is realistic.

Businesses that are unrealistically priced cannot be leveraged, nor will they sell.

Many businesses on the market are priced incorrectly. When an owner spends a lifetime building a business and decides to sell, the price is more often determined by the drudgery rather than the achievement. A business broker, on the other hand, generally calculates value based on some formulation, often computer produced. Brokers do not agree on a common method of appraisal, but the rule of thumb suggested above (a multiple of earnings) should prove adequate for both buyer and seller. High tech companies do not follow this rule; neither do heavy equipment and heavy shop companies. When asset values are way out of proportion to revenues, an evaluation in accordance with earnings may not be enough. The wise alternative is to steer clear of operations heavy in assets and sequential debt.

Calculate the selling price of a business by multiplying the adjusted earnings times three; four maximum.

Cash Required to Close

A buyer must negotiate terms and conditions conducive to the NBP methodology. Cash required to close and settle is a big consideration in so far as candidate selection. If the numbers fall within the established formulation, as numerous firms will, cash needs can be estimated. 50% to 60% of the selling price is the maximal objective. Any more may seriously expend the working capital; less could cause the seller to question the buyer's commitment to the deal.

In the example given above, 50% of $2,400,000 is $1,200,000. $1,200,000 is the cash required at closing to purchase the business. If the multiple times adjusted earnings had been 3, the cash required to settle would be $900,000. Sometimes, the more cash offered to the seller, the more negotiable the price becomes. If it is frugal, a buyer may offer more cash to bargain for a lower purchase price. A lower purchase price means less debt service.

In short, judicious buyers associated with the NBP, seek to find acquisition candidates which generate proven adjusted earnings 3% to 5%, or more, times revenue streams. The candidates are appraised to sell at a multiple of between three and four times adjusted earnings and require little more than 50% of the selling price in cash to close. A careful buyer may augment the last prerequisite when appropriate.

NOTE: In the real world, negotiations produce a variety of results. Where a buyer ends depends not only on skillful negotiations, but also chemistry and personal credibility with the seller. While one buyer contracts for 50% cash, another may not be able to get by with less than 70%. Some sellers will take back as much as 30% to 35% ownership; others will take none. Notes and earn-outs might be for as little as 5% of the total package, or as high as 50%, even more. Luck and faith also play a part.

Another example to study. Say the revenue of a construction company is $10,000,000 per year and expected to increase to $12,000,000 in the coming year. What is the math?

First, forget the increase in so far as calculating expected earnings or the selling price. A buyer may or may not be able to implement projected revenue increases. Adjusted earnings are estimated to be between $300,000 and $500,000. Selling price on the former should be somewhere between $900,000 to $1,200,000 and the latter between $1,500,000 and $2,000,000. Cash requirements on the former might fall at $450,000; $750,000 on the latter.

Debt Service

What about debt service? Post-closing, will the company be able to provide sufficient capital to pay debt?

Using the same numbers from the last illustration, the earnings are expected to be between $300,000 and $500,000 annually. In the former, the monthly average earnings are $25,000; in the latter, $41,667. Always presume a worst case scenario when calculating debt service. Normally, factoring will cost at least 2% per month; seller financing about 1% per month. Since there should be an even split between what the seller provides and what the assets will cost to leverage, one and 1/2% is the average debt service cost. The actual cost may not be that high. Therefore, on a monthly basis, one and 1/2% times the debt should equal the expected cost of debt service.

At $900,000, the monthly fee for debt service is $13,500. At $1,200,000, the monthly cost is $18,000. Yearly, the former totals $162,000; the latter totals $216,000. When a buyer keeps debt service fees at 50% of predicted earnings, supposedly there is sufficient margin for error. The former debt service calculation is a little more than 50%; the latter, a little less. Principal is not considered in this example.

Note: Receivables, when factored, turn over time after time and the advances made against the invoices may never be paid in full unless extreme budgetary controls are in place, an issue to be discussed later. For seller financing, the principal must be considered. However, at least 50% of the seller financing arrangement is expected to be in the form of an earn-out, another NBP methodology to be discussed later.

For purposes here, it is probably not erroneous to presume - to complete the math projections anyway - that one and 1/2% times the total purchase price per month represents a cautious debt service number.

Here's a Real Example with some Twists

By way of illustration, here is an example of a real operation to study. The company represents some very common problems that appear when how to finance is not apparent.

The company is located in the south; call it ABC. ABC had been in business for almost five decades, performed well and is debt free. The sellers had established a price that was non-negotiable: $7,500,000. The stockholder equity was not close to the asking price, nor was an acceptable multiple times earnings. For years, management had failed to figure out how to buy out the seller.

The revenue averaged less than $2,000,000 per month; cash on hand was not part of the sale; receivables averaged $2,000,000; inventory averaged about $4,000,000; and, adjusted earnings were stated at something less than $1,500,000. Stockholder equity was $4,500,000. A high quality broker - perhaps the best in the east - managed the deal.

Since the company had been financially solid for years, management was motivated to buy the company. They ran the company and had done so for years. Profit levels were extremely consistent. There was certainly a motivation to find a way to do the deal, but financing, as is often the case, was the major hang-up.

The local banks were reluctant to commit on the financing, not because of the track record of the company, or the management team, but by reason of the particular industry in which the business operated. Lenders over the country had been burnt and few were eager to participate. Bank financing had not been a particularly strong consideration.

The financing would therefore have to come from sources other than traditional sources. The task was monumental. None of the management personnel had any money to speak of, at least not the millions required to finance the sale, and the seller balked at any offer short of $7,500,000. Working capital would also have to be displayed by the buyer. The seller intended to take the operating cash at the time of closing yet did not want the management team to run short after a closing. Easy to see why the team had been unable to come up with the financing.

After weeks of thought, here is what I determined to be the best course of action:

1. Persuade the sellers to participate in an earn-out arrangement for the difference between the selling price and the equity of the company. The argument was mathematical and surprisingly acceptable. The management would also partake of the earn-out arrangement via a bonus plan. Thus seller thought that the earn-out was not only attainable, but also somewhat protected. $2,500,000 was in the till. $4,500,000 remained plus working capital. The seller required $500,000 working capital to close. Management would somehow have to come up with the cash.

2. The seller agreed to take back an unsecured short-term note for $300,000. An above market interest rate was offered as inducement.

3. As most will find, during the due diligence period, there are discrepancies between what has been reported as the value of the assets and what has been researched by the buyer. A quick rule of thumb is to calculate about 5% as an overstatement of value. The total assets here were about $5,000,000 so 5% times the same is $250,000. No problem from the seller.

The total collected to this point was $3,050,000. $4,450,000 plus $500,000 working capital remained to find.

4. The seller was further persuaded to take all the receivables as opposed to the management team having to factor them and losing at least 20% of the value. Factors usually advance only 80% of the receivable value. Since a trustworthy factor had committed to continuously factor all future receivables at a permissible rate, the need to keep the receivables on hand diminished.

Another $2,000,000 was in the bank. $2,450,000 plus $500,000 working capital left to fund. We were getting close, but the rest of the money required digging deep into my bag of tricks. Attentive readers will learn many of them.

5. Prefaced on an escrow closing and payable cycling (later chapters), Controlled Daily Balance, a process used to manage cash, was employed. The CDB process yields moderately dependable 15% times the average monthly revenue stream. Historical mathematical performance and pure logic convinced the seller that a 15% cash balance was more than realistic.

Another $300,000 bit the dust. $2,150,000 plus working capital to go.

6. The brokerage commission delay tactic worked, too. Readers will learn about the method later. The commission payment was delayed until after closing. Another NBP tactic worked. $300,000 more.

7. ABC had a glut of inventory. When measured by an unbiased outsider, the overage was in fact substantial. $500,000 of the stock was agreed a conservative amount of inventory to return. No argument; it should have been done a long time ago. In addition, while on the subject of inventory, $400,000 worth of inventory could be returned and repurchased later. $400,000 savings would be realized during an escrow closing within a 30 day period. The savings come when the payables due on that portion of stock disappear.

Another $900,000. With the broker's commission, the dollar shortage to close had been reduced to $950,000 plus $500,000 working capital. Progress in action. Few at ABC could believe it; never had anyone looked at what was obvious. The NBP works.

8. Equipment leaseback arrangements brought in another $350,000 and the cost to service the debt was in line with adjusted earnings.

No additional debt is proposed if the associated debt service cannot be covered.

9. The virtual corporation concept - explained in a later chapter - gave birth to the founding of an employee leaseback adaptation. An established employee-leasing firm agreed to become part of the process by taking the existing employees and leasing them back to ABC. That way an invoice could be generated and sold. In the first 30 days the payroll savings would surpass several hundred thousand dollars. $950,000 was wiped out and adjusted earnings thought conservative by management were more than ample to service the connected debt service. Sufficient profits remained. Now all that was left to find was $500,000 working capital.

10. The working capital was easy enough to find. There were many natural avenues yet to cross. After reading the balance of this writing, you find it! There is at least $2,500,000 left!

By the way, debt service incurred was easily offset by a reduction in operating expenses.

Buy That Business ... Poor old Daddy didn't Leave you!

Chapter Six: More Real-Life Examples

I received a list of businesses for sale from a large respected brokerage firm. Most of the opportunities are located in the west and mid-western regions of the United States. Over half have no suggested value attached, simply a note stating that an offer is expected. The ones that have asking prices shown are as follow:

1. A commercial roofing company with sales of $8,800,000, adjusted earnings of $740,000 and a value placed at $3,100,000.

2. A design/build commercial contractor with sales of $40,000,000, adjusted earnings of $750,000 and a value placed at $2,500,000.

3. A manufacturer/distributor of interior window coverings with sales of $4,574.000, adjusted earnings of $528,000 and a value placed at $1,500.000.

4. A manufacturer of vinyl covers with sales of $800,000, adjusted earnings of $220,000 and a value placed at $400,000.

5. A delivery courier with sales of $1,786,000, adjusted earnings of $340,000 and a value placed at $890,000.

6. Retail soccer stores with sales of $2,600,000, adjusted earnings of 365,000 and a value placed at $950,000.

7. A retail furniture and appliance store with sales of $1,840,000, adjusted earnings of $356,000 and a value placed at $1,200,000.

8. A mortgage broker/banker with sales of $800,000, adjusted earnings of $358,000 and a value placed at $850,000.

9. A car wash with sales of $732,000, adjusted earnings of $200,000 and a value place at $900,000.

What is learned from the aforementioned list?

First, the smaller the company the greater the value relative to sales. Larger companies are thus more suited to the Natural Business Philosophy's emphasis on cash flow management. The initial three businesses might fit the NBP standards more so than the last six entries.

Second, average adjusted earnings when compared to asking price (value) are about 1/3. Three is the general multiple used to determine value. The first three companies range from 2.8 to 4.1 and average about 3.4. The asking price is what it is; an asking price, and the adjusted earnings are subject to due diligence. These two points will affect the multiple.

Third, as to a buyer's ability to perform financially the first two businesses best fit the NBP criteria.

Business number one: If the asking price is negotiated to say 90% or $2,790,000, cash due at closing may be as little as $1,395,000. With monthly revenues averaging $733,000, CDB is $110,000, commission is probably $115,000 and 80% times one and one-half month's estimated receivables equates to another $880,000 - a total of $1,105,000. $290,000 plus closing and working capital expenses to go. We have only just begun.

Number two: If the asking price is negotiated to say 90% or $2,250,000, cash due at closing may be as little as $1,125,000. With monthly revenues averaging $3,333,000, CDB is $500,000. Commission is probably another $100,000 and receivables will probably provide the bulk of the balance.

Number three: If the asking price is negotiated to say 90% or $1,350,000, cash due at closing may be as little as $675,000. With monthly revenues averaging $353,000, CDB is $53,000. Commission is probably another $64,000 and 80% times one and one-half month's estimated receivables equates to another $425,000 - a total of $542,000. There is going to have to be more research to determine whether this company can be financed.

More actual businesses for sale to study

1. Book distributor with sales of $4,246,000 and adjusted earnings of $525,000.

2. Manufacturer and distributor of propellants and explosives with sales of $10,000,000 and adjusted earnings of $1,000,000.

3. Nationally distributed adult newspaper with sales of $800,000 and adjusted earnings of $212,000.

4. Sportswear manufacturing company with sales of $11,300,000 and adjusted earnings of $1,500,000.

5. Transportation services firm with sales of $1,133,000 and adjusted earnings of $439,000.

6. Telecommunication products and services with sales of $3,586,000 and adjusted earnings of $428,000.

7. Specialty trucking firm with sales of $10,000,000 and adjusted earnings of $2,000,000.

8. Wireless communication products with sales of $3,853,000 and adjusted earnings of $568,000.

9. Ranch, feed and equestrian supply with sales of $4,835,000 and adjusted earnings of $251,000.

10. Automated ticket/control systems with sales of $1,400,000 and adjusted earnings of $380,000.

11. Gifts and decorative accessories shop with sales of $1,313,000 and adjusted earnings of $280,000.

12. Wholesale beverage distributor with sales of $16,658,000 and adjusted earnings of $ 1,055,000.

13. Computer enterprise systems support service with sales of $4,000,000 and adjusted earnings of $1,250,000.

14. Medical professional placement agency with sales of $6,960,000 and adjusted earnings of $345,000.

15. Car wash with sales of $732,000 and adjusted earnings of $200,000.

16. Software consulting firm with sales of $4,000,000 and adjusted earnings of $847,000.

17. National interior design firm with sales of $6,500,000 and adjusted earnings of $725,000.

18. Computer training firm with sales of $4,309,000 and adjusted earnings of $316,000.

From the scanty information provided by the brokerage firm, there is much that the reader can glean as to a buyer's financial ability to perform. For example, if the multiple 'three to four times earnings equates to asking price applies, many of the companies listed are potential candidates for purchase. Of course there are many other considerations, but the first and most important aspect to take into account is money: Can the buyer perform? Miss this point and no matter how good the company is, forget it.

Let us take each one and study the potentials

1. Book distributor with sales of $4,246,000 and adjusted earnings of $525,000. A multiple of three equates to a selling price of $1,575,000. 50% cash at closing is $787,500 (plus closing costs and working capital needs).

Because of the business of distribution, I suspect that a three multiple is high; more likely 2. A two multiple reduces the estimated cash requirement to $525,000. When the average monthly revenue is about equal to the estimated cash require to close, more than likely the financing can be put in place. The reason for this presumption is this: CDB represents a potential 15% right from the start; receivables are another 80% anyway; inventory returned may add to the pile; and, commission delays bring some more. In time, readers will be able to figure the rest.

2. Manufacturer and distributor of propellants and explosives with sales of $10,000,000 and adjusted earnings of $1,000,000. A multiple of three equates to a selling price of $3,000,000. 50% cash at closing is $1,500,000 (plus closing costs and working capital needs).

This one doesn't even sound good. Yet, if only $1,500,000 is required to close the deal, there is a good chance that by applying the processes found in the Natural Business Philosophy the cash can be raised. There is probably an ample stockpile of inventory - it's a manufacturer - and combined with monthly revenue approaching $1,000,000, the receivables might come close to meeting the cash requirement. If not, a closer look at the financial statements will ascertain whether to pursue the candidate.

3. Nationally distributed adult newspaper with sales of $800,000 and adjusted earnings of $212,000. A multiple of three equates to a selling price of $636,000. 50% cash at closing is $318,000 (plus closing costs and working capital needs).

An adult newspaper is not a consideration regardless of the profit potential and ease of financing. Business is tough enough without the added discomfort connected with legal matters associated with adult material. Not worth the bother.

4. Sportswear manufacturing company with sales of $11,300,000 and adjusted earnings of $1,500,000. A multiple of three equates to a selling price of $4,500,000. 50% cash at closing is $2,250,000 (plus closing costs and working capital needs).

Manufacturing concerns usually have inventory on hand, sometimes a stockpile. Also, there is often the presence of equipment. Both can be leveraged. To save cash flow, return the inventory and buy it back. The equipment may be suitable for a leaseback arrangement. Manufacturers most often have a supply of receivables. This company, as is the case of many manufacturing firms, normally can be leveraged. $2,250,000 may look like a lot of dollars when compared to the revenue stream, but probably represents an excess of receivables, inventory and equipment.

5. Transportation services firm with sales of $1,133,000 and adjusted earnings of $439,000. A multiple of three equates to a selling price of $1,317,000. 50% cash at closing is $658,500 (plus closing costs and working capital needs).

When the estimated selling price is equal to the gross sales, move on!

6. Telecommunication products and services with sales of $3,586,000 and adjusted earnings of $428,000. A multiple of three equates to a

selling price of $1,248,000. 50% cash at closing is $642,000 (plus closing costs and working capital needs).

Inventory is going to be a factor here and leverage against inventory is not always easy. In fact, it is often downright impossible to accomplish. One of my close associates is in the communication business and from his tales, potential buyers should be very wary. The communications industry is in a constant state of flux.

7. Specialty trucking firm with sales of $10,000,000 and adjusted earnings of $2,000,000. A multiple of three equates to a selling price of $6,000,000. 50% cash at closing is $3,000,000 (plus closing costs and working capital needs).

Having been involved with the trucking industry, the financial statements here will probably show a large equity gap. Even though the asking price is $6,000,000, there is a lot of equity in the equipment to leverage. Leaseback arrangements are not that hard to obtain if the company is established and management is proven. A leaseback-lending scenario might gain the buyer a large cash payment. When added to the potential to factor receivables - most common in the trucking business - cash requirements should be met.

Trucking is not an easy industry to operate without experience. Drivers and owner-operators move from one company to the next frequently. Trucking may sound exciting, but be careful!

8. Wireless communication products with sales of $3,853,000 and adjusted earnings of $568,000. A multiple of three equates to a selling price of $1,704,000. 50% cash at closing is $852,000 (plus closing costs and working capital needs).

Repeating, inventory is going to be a factor here and leverage against inventory is not always easy. In fact, it is often downright impossible to accomplish. One of my close associates is in the communication business and from his tales, potential buyers should be very wary. The communications industry is in a constant state of flux.

9. Ranch, feed and equestrian supply with sales of $4,835,000 and adjusted earnings of $251,000. A multiple of three equates to a selling price of $753,000. 50% cash at closing is $376,500 (plus closing costs and working capital needs).

I do not know anything about the feed business, but I suspect that potential buyers are not going to have a hard time financing this particular operation. From the brief information listed - subject of course to due diligence - the estimated cash requirement to close is easily obtained from CDB, receivable leverage and perhaps using a holding company. Corporate credit may affect the latter.

10. Automated ticket/control systems with sales of $1,400,000 and adjusted earnings of $380,000. A multiple of three equates to a selling price of $1,140,000. 50% cash at closing is $570,000 (plus closing costs and working capital needs).

Repeating, when the estimated selling price is almost equal to the gross sales, move on!

11. Gifts and decorative accessories shop with sales of $1,313,000 and adjusted earnings of $280,000. A multiple of three equates to a selling price of $840,000. 50% cash at closing is $420,000 (plus closing costs and working capital needs).

Inventory, inventory, inventory; that is the key word here. Better be a ton of seller financing, or the buyer is going to have to find a bank to leverage the inventory; tough to do.

12. Wholesale beverage distributor with gross sales of $16,658,000 and adjusted earnings of $1,055,000. A multiple of three equates to a selling price of $3,165,000. 50% cash at closing is $1,582,500 (plus closing costs and working capital needs).

On the surface, the earnings sound high. Typical distributors operate on rather low margins and adjusted earnings of $1,055,000 are unusually high. Yet, if the operation is mom and pop vintage, which it surely is, there should be many benefits to any owner. Beware that such benefits may not pass to a buyer, especially if the buyer is in an expansion mode. That involves greater expenses. A purchase price in the $3,000,000 range will result in substantial debt service. There is much that must be learned from the financial statements of this business and a personal visit. On first glance, it is not a candidate to consider.

13. Computer enterprise systems support service with sales of $4,000,000 and adjusted earnings of $1,250,000. A multiple of three equates to a selling price of $3,750,000. 50% cash at closing is $1,875,000 (plus closing costs and working capital needs).

Traditionally, high tech companies are not priced at a multiple of three; more likely five to ten. No matter the multiple, this particular operation would probably not fall within the guidelines necessary to fully exploit the Natural Business Philosophy processes. Buyers better have deep pockets in these cases; not worth the bother?

14. Medical professional placement agency with sales of $6,960,000 and adjusted earnings of $345,000. A multiple of three equates to a selling price of $1,035,000. 50% cash at closing is $517,500 (plus closing costs and working capital needs).

Employment agencies are tough to operate, just ask anyone who does. The profits are normally low and generally. Unless buyers are experienced, better pass the opportunity. However this particular business is probably capable of leverage. The estimated cash required to close is about equal to the average monthly revenue stream - which is good. Also the multiple - two - is probably high.

15. Car wash with sales of $732,000 and adjusted earnings of $200,000. A multiple of three equates to a selling price of $600,000. 50% cash at closing is $300,000 (plus closing costs and working capital needs).

Unless the real estate warrants borrowing a substantial portion of the cash required to close, the NBP may not be able to leverage ample cash. This company is an example of low revenue, high price. A revenue near the selling price is very difficult to leverage. Such operations are usually one person and not of the sort recommended to acquire.

16. Software consulting firm with sales of $4,000,000 and adjusted earnings of $847,000. A multiple of three equates to a selling price of $2,541,000. 50% cash at closing is $1,270,500 (plus closing costs and working capital needs).

Repeating, high tech companies are not priced at a multiple of three; more likely five to ten. No matter the multiple, this particular operation would probably not fall within the guidelines necessary to exploit fully the Natural Business Philosophy processes. Buyers better have deep pockets in these cases; not worth the bother?

17. National interior design firm with sales of $6,500,000 and adjusted earnings of $725,000. A multiple of three equates to a selling price of $2,175,000. 50% cash at closing is $1,087,500 (plus closing costs and working capital needs).

On the surface, it appears that this company may be difficult to finance. On closer examination, financing is elementary. I happen to know this one and have already examined the financials. The company is very solid with an excellent national reputation and good management. The reason for selling is acceptable. Financial statements show that the receivables in combination with inventory, CDB and a seller's note are more than sufficient to finance the purchase.

18.   Computer training firm with sales of $4,309,000 and adjusted earnings of $316,000. A multiple of three equates to a selling price of $948,000. 50% cash at closing is $474,000 (plus closing costs and working capital needs).

Repeating once more, high tech companies are not priced at a multiple of three; more likely five to ten. No matter the multiple, this particular operation would probably not fall within the guidelines necessary to exploit fully the Natural Business Philosophy processes. Buyers better have deep pockets in these cases; not worth the bother?

After first glancing at the above businesses for sale, few potential opportunities appear, but a second glance and some personal background experiences bring five to six probabilities. The longer a buyer is in the market, the more candidates he or she will discover. Keep in mind though that the information here is limited. Buyers need to get hold of corporate financials to study.

Even restricted data provides insight into a possible candidate's potential. To take the time to visit all the operations listed would take months. Save time and energy by gathering insight from what is offered by a broker and from what is obtained after a non-disclosure document is signed. If after brief examination of the corporate financials, the business for sale still looks promising, take a trip.

Buy That Business ... Poor old Daddy didn't Leave you!

Chapter Seven: Negotiations

Seldom will a candidate be acceptable for purchase consideration on first glance. Usually, the asking price is too high, or the seller terms unreasonable, or the company financials are recast incorrectly. Do not be discouraged, if after looking at dozens of companies for sale, none of them come up to standard. Once negotiations begin, it is surprising how many of the candidates suddenly take on new hope.

Bargaining and Lawyers

Bargaining is both fun and stressful. Since there is a lot riding on who wins the best deal at the table, the players quickly forget that the world will not end should either party win a little here, lose a little there. Get an attorney involved and the pressure increases. A lawyer is traditionally known as a deal killer, not so much out of conservatism or correctness, but more so out of learned technique and habit. No matter what, the opponent is wrong. Let's get him!

A buyer will need an attorney to close the deal, but keep the lawyer away from the bargaining table.

The Game Rules

Regardless of who is doing the negotiations, or the mood of the bargaining, there are certain basic rules to follow when it comes to terms and conditions. One quickly comes to mind: Whatever the price, keep the cash requirement to close at 50% or less. Second, the seller should have little problem holding a note for 25% of the selling price. Often the security for the note is corporate stock. If the buyer defaults, the seller gets back into the company. A personal signature may be required, but credit is rarely the criteria. Third, an earn-out arrangement in the area of 25% times the purchase price is reasonable.

Thus, purchase prices paid with 50% or less in cash, a seller's note for 25% and an earn-out arrangement for another 25% are the goals.

Get Help

If this is the buyer's first acquisition experience, get some help, or get eaten alive. With an experienced business broker or the seller's attorney, the odds that a first-time buyer will ever get to the closing table are slim to none. No seller is going to turnover an established operation to a novice with big aspirations, but no experience. Even if the buyer gets the capital through the prudent application of the NBP, a sane seller, no matter how confident the buyer, will push away from the table. When this happens, a second chance is rarely given.

Get help on deal number one.

Ability to Perform

Can the buyer perform? In other words, can the buyer bring the required purchase dollars to the closing table? After closing, can the buyer operate the business successfully? The seller, the seller's attorney, and the seller's business broker each want to know. Big questions. A seasoned owner and management team members may be able to answer correctly, but an unknown entrepreneur may not. Credible answers are necessary to play in the corporate acquisition game.

A seasoned owner of an existing business has little problem with these questions; neither does an experienced management team. They either have the money, or they do not. They usually have the proven know-how to run an operation successfully, or they would not be at the bargaining table in the first place.

In the instance of a management team, most often I have found that the big problem is money. No matter what the desire or experience level, money to buy the business is often lacking. Many management groups are unable to buy the company in which they work, perhaps built, because they cannot figure out how to raise the cash.

The same goes for an owner who wants to expand business. He or she may have the necessary qualifications for achievement, but lacks the money to buy another business.

The Natural Business Philosophy is absolutely made for management teams who want to buy out their bosses and for existing business owners who seek to expand their operations. The Natural Business Philosophy is also ideal for ambitious entrepreneurs who need an acquisition. Yet, how can an entrepreneur gain sufficient credibility to persuade a seller to sell? Where can a management team or an owner of an existing business get the money?

How can an ambitious entrepreneur acquire a business? Find experienced help. Where? How about the management team in place, or an owner of another business entity in search of growth? Is that not a natural way to bring to the table what is missing? If credibility is what the seller desires, give it. Talk to the management team in place or find a local somebody who will come along for the ride. Everyone benefits. Accomplish that and closing is only steps away. Money is all that is necessary now and guess what? That is the idea behind this writing - how to get the money.

Here is another way to bring the seller to the table if an unseasoned business person is beckoning: Pre-finance the deal. However, to pre-finance a purchase before a contract is signed represents a huge gamble, especially if the seller refuses to turn over necessary financial information without an agreement in hand. There are going to be expenses, commitments and a whole lot of time and effort involved. How can a buyer get to the financing stage before a contract is signed? Without financing, what good is a contract anyway?

Draft a letter of intent. Draft a letter of intent to the seller outlining whatever the intentions are in regard to the purchase of the company. Often a seller will sign a short-term letter of intent just to test the waters. No obligation occurs and if the buyer finds financing, credibility grows. With financing in hand, any buyer can move forward.

Draft a letter of intent.

A letter of intent is simply a letter written from one company to another - or one person to a company - acknowledging a willingness to do business along with an ability to do business. It is a letter written during the first stages of a potential transaction. Usually drafted by the buyer, a letter of intent contains specific terms and conditions relevant to the proposed transaction. The letter acknowledges that further negotiations are necessary to close and settle.

A letter of intent begins to help insure each party that there is a definite interest to proceed with negotiations to close the deal. The seller is now on record to sell; the buyer is now on record to buy. A meeting of the minds has been reached on certain key issues. The all-important first step has been taken. Effectively, the initiation of a letter of intent produces a worthy commitment to proceed in good faith to the bargaining table. Each party to the letter is now charged with the responsibility to invest resources to bring the transaction to closure.

Know this: A letter of intent, whether deliberately or through ignorance, may legally bind the parties to certain transaction terms and conditions. Even though terms and conditions are denoted in the letter as nonbinding, it may be impractical for a party to a potential transaction to renegotiate these terms should the necessity arise. Trustworthiness and a sense of commitment between the parties are key components to a letter of intent. Once reached, this mutual commitment makes it difficult to later tamper with the provisions.

Also the time necessary to negotiate the deal points that will eventually lead to a letter of intent might be more wisely employed fighting through a definitive purchase agreement. Make the letter a lightweight document. A final agreement to close a transaction is delayed or even lost when too much time is spent in the negotiation period required to formulate a letter of intent.

A letter of intent contains a description of the business or assets to be purchased along with the structure of the transaction. Is it going to be a purchase of corporate assets, corporate stock or a merger arrangement? To clearly define the parties to the potential transaction is appropriate, too.

Terms of payment are critical and must be stated clearly. Include anticipated seller financing, or extended earn-out arrangements, security issues and any other considerations that are required to close the deal.

To prevent the seller from selling to another party, the purchaser often adds a no-shop clause. The buyer then feels some degree of comfort knowing, at least for an agreed on time period, that the time, effort and money to be spent during the acquisition process will not be in vain.

Due diligence, financing, drafting a definitive purchase agreement, developing management contracts and other responsibilities essential to close a purchase require time. A letter of intent should fix the time period during which a purchaser accomplishes what is required to start a proper closing and settlement. It also sets the fixed time by which the definitive purchase agreement must be executed if the transaction is to close.

A letter of intent shall also mention certain contingencies. For example, to close, certain key employees must contract to remain with

63

the company. Another such contingency may require the seller to enter into a non-compete contract with the buyer.

Contained in the letter will be the assumption of specified corporate liabilities such as the payables. All assets to be assumed by the buyer are to be mentioned. Also to be contained in the letter: How business will be conducted during the interim before closing, including the payment of expenses; public disclosure of the pending sale to appropriate parties associated with the corporation; governing law; reimbursement of associated expenses; and, some words showing that the definitive purchase agreement is the only ruling and binding agreement. The latter is subject to any provision in the letter of intent that is meant otherwise.

To insure that the other terms of the letter are nonbinding and negotiable, the letter of intent should assert that the terms and conditions stated, unless otherwise noted, are subject to negotiation and the implementation of a definitive purchase agreement.

A letter of intent should contain an obligation by the parties to bargain in good faith, termination dates of the events described and permission by the corporation to allow the buyer access to the corporate records.

A letter of intent opens the door to look at the financials, especially the accounts receivable aging reports, a first request.

TRY TO NEGOTIATE FRONT COSTS AWAY

The cost to do a purchase is more than cash to close. There are expenses associated with appraisals, financial commitments, attorney and accounting fees, travel and so on. These costs are pretty high, especially if the deal does not close. $50,000 to $100,000 is normal. What to do?

Sometimes there is not much a buyer can do to avoid some of the associated costs. Take for example equipment appraisals. No professional is going to travel to a site and evaluate anything for free unless the appraiser is kin; sometimes not even then. A lawyer or CPA, generally part of any acquisition will not perform without pay either. Get a loan commitment and the cost to carry out due diligence is anywhere from $10,000 to $25,000. What if there is more than one candidate to consider? The cost is even more.

What I have done in the past is to eliminate some expenses and reduce others through firm negotiation. Lucky for me that I found an attorney and CPA willing to gamble a little. If the purchase looks relatively certain to close, they will wait until closing for payment of services. There are others in the profession who will also cooperate with a buyer who has done adequate homework and is able to prove it. To await pay is rewarding. Because fees to close an acquisition as a rule are higher than for typical clientele work.

Seldom have I ever paid front money on a contract. Tradition asks for a little money on the table to bind the agreement and show good faith. What is there to lose if no money hits the hands of the seller? Most brokers will require escrow cash.

If the matter comes up, I simply have my attorney call the broker and relate in detail all the expected expenses paid out before and after entry into the contract: Attorney and CPA costs, financial commitment costs, personal time and effort, appraisal fees, travel, consultation, and etc. When all the expenses are added together, there is reasonable argument that the escrow requirement be waived. If not, do not quit. Cut the amount due and pay as little as possible. Often I have timed the signing of the contract to occur at the same time as the closing. It works and thousands of dollars are saved!

Appraisal and financial commitment fees are harder to dismiss. However, the latter is very negotiable. Once I cut a fee from $25,000 to $5,000. When using a factor, there is usually no fee.

Whenever possible, negotiate away, or at least reduce front costs.

Chapter Eight: Receivable Financing

A Corporation's accounts receivable aging report is generally the first document to examine when seeking quick cash to buy a company. The aging report lists all the money due from clients of the corporation and how long each invoice has been outstanding. Where the debt is owed by a credit worthy company and is less than 90 days old, chances are good that the invoice might be sold to a factor. A factor is a lender who buys accounts receivable based on the credit of the receivable, not the holder of the receivable.

When sold, up to 80% of the amount due is advanced in cash. A receivable sale turns over ownership to the factor. When the invoice is paid, any balance due the corporation - known as the reserve (20% here) - is returned. The agreed on discount (fee) - generally one and 1/4 to four points per each 30 day period - is removed from the balance due. 96% to over 98% of the receivable is cashed.

If a corporation is owed a total of $1,000,000 from customers with good credit who pay timely (the clients pay invoices in 30 to 60 days), the holder of these receivables can sell them and receive an $800,000 cash advance. A buyer of this corporation may sell the receivables and use the funds at closing.

What is a Receivable?

First, a receivable is nothing more than a piece of paper termed an invoice that has been sent to a corporation's customer for services rendered, or a product delivered. An invoice does not become a receivable until the service has been performed, or the product has been delivered. Whether a service or product, performance or delivery must be verifiable. A factor will call the one who owes the debt and make sure that a receivable has been created (services have been rendered or a product has been delivered) and that there is no chance for dispute. Since the factor is going to take ownership of the receivable, any dispute will hamper collection. Thus, the receivable must be verifiable.

A receivable is an authenticated invoice sent to a customer for services rendered, or a product delivered.

A Receivable Stands Alone Credit-Wise

Second, receivables are instruments created by a corporation, but owed by another. When the debtor has a good credit rating and pays timely, the instrument becomes valuable regardless of the credit of its creator. The value of a receivable is weighed in favor of the one who owes the debt. Even if the creator of the instrument is a start-up company, or has less than perfect credit, its qualified receivables can be sold. Since a receivable stands alone in terms of credit, a buyer of a corporation with qualified receivables can also sell the receivables. A buyer of a company can thus sell the company's qualified receivables even if the buyer has little or no cash and credit.

The worth of a receivable is subject to the credit of the one who owes it.

Consider Only Unliened Receivables

Third, when seeking out a company to acquire, it makes sense to consider only those with qualified receivables. However, qualified receivables - from clients with good credit - are only half the battle. The invoices due must not be liened. If they are liened already, there is no further leverage to be had by a buyer. In some instances, a company for sale may have a bank line of credit in place. The local bank probably has a lien on the receivables and all other assets of the corporation. There is no room for additional leverage. Unless the circumstances are unusual, pass on any company that has a lien on its receivables.

To leverage a receivable, there can be no lien against that receivable.

Receivables must be Sufficient

Fourth, make sure that the total dollar amount of qualified receivables, when sold to a factor, will bring to closing sufficient dollars to make the transaction worth doing. The total dollar amount necessary is directly proportional to the amount of cash required to close the purchase of the company. In a typical acquisition scenario, the seller carries part of the purchase price and perhaps enters what is known as an earn-out arrangement. The former is simply a legal note secured to the seller's satisfaction. The latter is an agreement to further pay money to the seller under specific conditions. Whereas, the note must be paid or default is declared, an earn-out is contingent on the future performance of the corporation. The difference between what the seller agrees to hold and the negotiated purchase price for the business must be paid in cash at the closing. Thus, cash requirements to close on a purchased must be sufficiently offset by the sale of qualified receivables.

Adequate cash at closing is frequently dependent on the existing amount of qualified receivables.

45 Days of Qualified Receivables

Fifth, look for a business with at least 45 days' worth of qualified receivables usually on hand. 45 days receivables translate into about one and one-half months revenue. Revenue, as discussed later, plays a big part in a buyer's ability to raise cash. A business with monthly revenues averaging $1,000,000 should have on hand about $1,500,000 worth of receivables. Make sure they are qualified. $1,500,000 receivables bring $1,200,000 cash to the closing table.

Seek to purchase a corporation with at least 45 days' worth of qualified receivables on hand.

The Cost of Receivables

Sixth, factors are expensive, considerably more costly than a bank. Bank rates may be less than 1% per month (1% times the amount advanced against the receivable) versus a factoring rate of up to 5% per month. Usually, 5% is charged against 100% of the invoice amount, not the 80% advance, so the cost is steep. Factors have been around for a long time and are willing to take risks that banks refuse to accept - therefore the high fees. However, Fortune 500 companies use factors. Why? Because there is a need to quickly turn dollars without hassle. Many astute business operators have found how to best benefit by factoring.

Caution is the keyword, but a better word is shop. Shop around for the best rates. Factors are competitive and will negotiate. The Internet is maybe the most fertile arena in which to search for advantageous terms.

The best rate I have seen is one and 1/4% per month times the amount advanced. Yes, even that rate is a little higher than a normal bank, but there are no personal signatures required, no liens placed against the corporate assets and no long-term contracts. The process is quick, easy and cost efficient. Bottom line: Shop around for the best terms from a factor.

However, to reduce factoring fees, smart operators take discounts from venders and suppliers, or add a small contingency to invoices. Also, factoring is sometimes competitive when closing costs, origination fees and points are considered. Factoring uses much less collateral, requires minimal paperwork and is set in motion in a week or less.

Hunt for the best finance terms when working with a factor.

Give the Seller the Receivables

Seventh, an often-missed practice when negotiating an acquisition is to offer the seller, as part of the purchase price, all or part of the receivables. The seller in most instances must guarantee that all the receivables on hand at closing are collectable. The seller may even be required to deposit a certain amount of cash into an escrow account to insure collectability. So, why should the seller not take the receivables as part of the purchase price?

If the accounting numbers support the operation after closing - that is, working capital is sufficient, a line-of-credit is in place and receivable collection is generally timely - the buyer is able to put more cash into the deal if the seller takes the receivables as part of the selling price.

Here is the math: Only 80% is advanced in cash against qualified receivables. Should the seller be persuaded to take 100% of the receivables as part of the purchase price, then 100% of the receivables are credited against the cash requirement. There is a 20% gain in applicable cash.

Offer the seller, as part of the purchase price, all or part of the receivables.

Receivable Example

Here is an instance to illustrate how receivables affect the selling price of a business. The seller establishes the purchase price of his family-run operation at $4,500,000. The seller supposes that a buyer will leverage both the corporate receivables and inventory to gain a major portion of the purchase price. The balance is to come from outside investor cash. Sounds reasonable at first glance.

However, the industry in which the business operates is in general turmoil and several lenders have recently been burnt by advancing against what turned out to be less than qualified receivables and inventory. Although this particular business does well, banks frown on the collateral, particularly the receivables and inventory. Advance rates against receivables are dramatically reduced to 65%; advance rates against the inventory are cut from 50% to 35%. To make matters worse, some of the receivables are from foreign clients. They cannot be leveraged at all.

Receivables total about $2,000,000 and a full 50% are foreign. A best case scenario means that the cash availability is a low percentage times $1,000,000 or a whopping $650,000. Remember the sales price? $4,500,000. The probable advance available against receivables makes little impact against the purchase price. The first thought is to walk from the deal.

Common sense dictates that in this example the seller should take the $2,000,000 worth of invoices and thereby reduce the selling price accordingly. Instead of $4,500,000, the price becomes $2,500,000. Instead of borrowing $650,000 against the invoices - a wasteful act - a full credit of $2,000,000 is earned. No need to guarantee receivables and no need to borrow against them. Now that is common sense!

When possible and when the numbers work after closing, ask the seller to take 100% of the receivables as part of the purchase price.

About the Use of Factoring

Factoring dollars can help fund the purchase of a business, bolster inventory, help expand a stagnant operation and aid in the development of a long list of other financing opportunities. Also, factoring offers collection control and enables companies to extend credit terms to clients. Users can take advantage of volume discounts without giving up equity or incurring extra debt. Best of all, users leverage off customer's credit. Banks and investors are not necessary to fulfill money needs.

Receivables are factored once, or in part, or on a continuing basis. Factoring allows tremendous flexibility. Yet, keep in mind that when factoring is stripped of its high promise, it is nothing more than another way that a lender squeezes money from the business community.

Expenses and Other Details to Scrutinize

Factoring is expensive, often misunderstood, and might result in the ruination of a business. There are many hidden elements to scrutinize: Escrow funds, delays in reimbursement of balances owed, and fees charged against 100% of an invoice (not the 80% advanced). Working capital needs may be undercapitalized when only 80% of the receivables are available. Profits disappear and once caught up in the factoring cycle, poorly operated businesses might not be able to escape its hold.

Not too long ago, factoring was used to help liquefy the operations of two familiar businesses who operated in very competitive markets. In both instances, the companies quickly gave the impression that all bad had turned good. Within three months, each filed bankruptcy; not because of factoring, but due to the improper use of factoring. Factoring here was used as a life jacket in a sea of sharks, not a motor to put on the back of a slowly sinking boat to try to get it out of infested water.

The improper use of factoring might quickly ruin a poorly run business operation.

Buy That Business ... Poor old Daddy didn't Leave you!

Chapter Nine: Seller Financing

Seller financing is often the most crucial segment of the financial package presented by a potential buyer. Without some financial involvement by the seller in the funding of the purchase price, most small business acquisitions cannot take place. Even after taking into account what a typical lender might advance against receivables, inventory and other hard assets, there is usually a wide money gap yet to fill before a purchase can occur. Since an all cash contract from a buyer is unrealistic, the seller must step in and provide some financial help.

What is Seller Financing?

Seller financing means that the seller of the company, or major stockholder, is willing to hold a note for a portion of the purchase price. In other words, the seller is going to wait for part of the purchase price. Whether it is an employee from within, the management team, or a buyer from outside, the seller must be satisfied that any money due on the note will be paid in full and paid on time. The security for the note is generally the stock of the corporation held in escrow to insure that the seller can get back into the operation if the buyer defaults. Short of that, the seller may require a personal guarantee by the buyer, or additional collateral equal to the note. A secured seller thus cares little about default. The amount held by the seller varies, but can be as little as 10%, or as much as 70%. 50% is the average.

Seller Stays On

As part of the negotiations, a seller may increase the purchase price via a contract to remain in some capacity with the company. An agreement to act as either a consultant or, as a part of management, is standard. Hours may be restricted and the wages for services intentionally a bit high, but the buyer can benefit from the seller's involvement in several ways.

First, there is an ongoing operational confidence when the seller remains aboard, particularly right after closing. Clients and employees are more comfortable with the presence of someone they know and trust.

Second, the buyer is able to cut some of the purchase dollars by employing the seller under terms monetarily advantageous to the seller.

Third, the seller is paid out of the company till, not out of buyer funds. On the other hand, if money is due, the seller is able to keep an eye on things for a time without the headaches previously endured.

Seller Earn-out

Perhaps the best financing package of all is the seller earn-out arrangement. An earn-out is a contract between the seller and buyer which offers the seller an opportunity to gain more dollars for the company without penalizing the buyer. The buyer requires less money up front, but under negotiated terms and conditions, the seller receives more money over time.

For example, say that the buyer and seller agree that should the company continue to grow over the next five years, there shall be a 50-50 split of all earnings greater than those existing at closing. If at closing, earnings before interest, taxes, depreciation and amortization (EBITDA) are $250,000, then at the end of year one post-closing, audited profits of $300,000 generate another $25,000 for the seller. Over a five-year period, the seller stands to earn a lot of money.

An earn-out is customarily packaged along with an employment contract to grant the seller continued input into the operation. Earn-out dollars are consequently more likely to be achieved. Without some medium of influence, the buyer may obstruct, even innocently, the seller's ability to make the earn-out.

In short, the earn-out provides the seller with an opportunity to continue receiving income after the sale without placing disproportionate financial burdens on the buyer. Tax advantages might also be realized through the formulation of a carefully devised earn-out plan.

A skillful buyer will always attempt to negotiate a reasonable note and earn-out position with the seller.

Employment Contract

An employment contract is an agreement with either the seller or key members of the management team, or both. The engagement is for as long as negotiated and generally considered part of the selling price. Here are some, but not all of the details to include in an employment contract:

1. Employment. What are the position and duties of the employee?

2. Term. What will be the term of employment?

3. Time. What time and effort will be required by the employee?

4. Office Space. What office space will be provided?

5. Compensation. Including notes and earn-out terms, what are the terms and conditions attached to the compensation package?

6. Termination. How can either party terminate this Agreement? What affect will termination have on compensation?

7. Renewal. What will occur when this Agreement expires?

8. Policies. What are the employer's general operating policies?

9. Vacation. How is vacation defined?

10. Expenses. What expenses are compensated and what expenses are not?

11. Memberships. What membership privileges are paid by the employer?

12. Insurances and 401k. What insurances and saving plans are available?

13. Automobile. What are the terms and conditions associated with a company vehicle?

14. Short-term Sickness. What is the definition of a sick day?

15. Prolonged Illness or Accident. How will prolonged illnesses or accidents be compensated?

16. Restrictive Covenant. What are the terms and conditions of a non-compete Agreement?

17. Arbitration of Controversies. How will any claim or controversy be handled?

The Flip Side

Simply to get the seller to carry more of the financial obligation is not always wise. Diminishing the amount of cash required to close is the aim, but seller financing can bring the seller into your face for an extended period of time. Such influence can indirectly push the company toward a course harmful to the goals of the buyer. Too, the cost of seller financing can sometimes be greater than the cost of other more conventional methods. And, with an earn-out, the buyer is obligated to share profit expansion even if the growth comes not by the seller, but as a result of the buyer's hard work.

Bargain with the seller to hold part of the purchase price, 50% is the goal. More may be detrimental. Less may make the acquisition impossible, especially without an investor, or heavy bank backing. The goal is to avoid or eliminate investor input. Investors can often be even more unreasonable than sellers can.

Buy That Business ... Poor old Daddy didn't Leave you!

Chapter Ten: Controlled Daily Balance

When a business regularly pays its bills (payables), checks are written for the amount due and sent to the one owed money. A check is simply a draft instrument that grants to the one owed money the right to go to a bank and exchange the check for cash. Most checks however are not cashed, but instead are deposited into the account of the holder. The bank then processes the check and in a day or so the bank on which the check is drawn mechanically withdraws cash from the sender.

The process whereby one business receives revenue from another and pays out payables continues on and on from one entity to another. Each time revenue is received and payables paid in this fashion, new money is generated. It's the same money, of course, but it is recognized as new money. A bank involved with each piece of the process sees the same money over and over. The bank benefits from the cash flow and uses the fleeting money to its advantage.

Writing, sending, depositing and processing checks are business and banking operations that create fluctuating balances in both the corporate checkbook and that at the bank. What is shown at the bank is seldom what is written at the corporation level. The bank uses depositor's money and is thus interested in how much is going to be deposited by each of its business customers over any given 30-day period. The more money received, and the longer the bank holds on to the money, the greater its opportunity to benefit from its usage.

Trace a Dollar Bill

To better illustrate how this operation performs, look first at an uncomplicated version of how cash is created and how it flows:

Imagine that three candy stores - A, B and C - are located on Main Street in Small Town, USA. A customer walks into the first store and buys a chocolate candy bar for $1.00. The owner of this store, candy store A, takes the dollar bill from the customer and immediately walks out of store A and skips on down the street to store B. There in store B, the owner of store A buys a vanilla candy bar for $1.00 and gives the owner of store B the dollar bill.

Then the owner of store B walks out onto Main Street and strolls down the sidewalk to store C. The owner of store B buys a peanut butter candy bar at store C and pays for the candy bar with the same dollar bill received from the owner of store A.

A single dollar bill is traced from point A to point B to point C. The process is simple, as it should be. Cash is exchanged for a product. Each time the exchange occurs, new money is created. New money does not mean money just printed, but money regenerated. In all, the same $1.00 bill purchased three candy bars. Each store records revenue of $1.00. If each candy bar costs $.50, $.50 is paid to a wholesaler. $3.00 is spent retail. $1.50 is spent wholesale. Taxes are based on profits made on $3.00.

Immediately evident is why it is important to understand how cash flows and how cash flow affects a company's revenue. Many small business owners fail to grasp the full impact of how money is created, how it flows and what it means to each stop as it flows. When a bank gets hold of depositor's money, the bank uses the money. Loans are extended, investments are made and employees are paid.

Just like a bank, businesses receive cash. A business person who is knowledgeable about cash flow will delay the flow of money as long as possible. That way the business can take advantage of the cash as it hits the till - just like a bank.

Trace a Million Dollars

Revenues flow from one entity through another in the normal course of conducting business. The following simplistic illustration shows how a cash steam might flow from a sales organization through a wholesale company and finally into a manufacturing concern. Each uses the same bank. The timing of payables and receipt of revenues are important.

Sales, Inc. receives revenue from customers that total $1,000,000. $800,000.00 is reserved to pay cost of goods owed to Wholesaler, Inc. The balance - $200,000 - is set aside to pay overhead and other corporate expenses. Sales, Inc.'s customers pay for products with cash or charge card. Charges are reimbursed within three days. No credit is extended.

Wholesaler, Inc. receives $800,000 revenue from Sales, Inc. Wholesaler, Inc. then earmarks $640,000 to pay Manufacturing, Inc. Sales, Inc. pays in 30 days.

Continuing the cycle, Manufacturing, Inc. receives $640,000 revenue from Wholesaler, Inc. Manufacturing, Inc. allocates $512,000.00 to cover its cost of goods. Wholesaler, Inc. pays in 30 days.

In reverse order, Manufacturing, Inc. sells its product to Wholesale, Inc. Sales, Inc. then purchases its products from Wholesale, Inc. Which comes first? Payables, receivables, or revenues? The answer is important as it varies with each operation. All are part and parcel of the same cycle and instrumental to the understanding of good cash management. The NBP understands how the cycle works. Readers must understand it too. Reread this chapter.

Wholesale, Inc. will in all likelihood have to carry a stockpile of inventory; Sales, Inc. should have the most liquid operation; and,

Manufacturing, Inc. may have to wait up to 60 days to collect receivables.

As in the story about candy bars, where $1.00 turns into $3.00, when the revenue generated by Sales, Inc., Wholesaler, Inc. and Manufacturing, Inc. are added together, $1,000,000 becomes $2,440,000. If each corporation uses the same bank, astute readers already know how the bank benefits..

Corporate Daily Balance and Bank Daily Balance

Average daily balance is a banking term which denotes the typical dollar balance in a customer's account during a given month. A business with monthly revenues of $100,000 may have days when there is zero balance, and days when there is as much as $10,000 shown on the bank records. The average of all the balances during a given 30-day period may be $5,000, thus an average daily balance of $5,000.

On the other hand, the same corporation that shows an average daily balance of $5,000 at the bank may actually show zero in the corporate checkbook. In fact, the book may show a negative balance. The bank does not know what checks are written, only those that have been received and processed. Bank balances are thus not an accurate picture of a corporation's cash on hand. If the corporate checkbook balance is zero and the balance at the bank is $5,000, the $5,000 is termed float. Float no longer exists in so far as the corporation is concerned and cannot be counted as an asset even though it shows up at the bank as real cash. The bank is the only beneficiary.

As elementary as it may seem, most business owners do not know how money is generated, how it flows and how it is best managed. Some do not even differentiate between daily balance and average daily balance. They spend company funds as if there was an endless supply of money, even if their corporate checkbooks show that funds are depleted.

While there is money on the bank ledger, the check writing continues. Checks bounce and more checks are written. Some businesses make a business paying invoices by writing check after check, holding this one, or that one and making deposits at the last moment.

Some operations are so tight financially that the only way to stay in business is to run negative bank balances, hold checks, make false promises to vendors, or simply bounce checks and catch up later. Sooner or later, this method of operating catches up to the owner and the business simply collapses from the absence of financial stability.

Capture Maximum Dollars

One of the most formidable financial tools ever devised is not a tool at all. It is an understanding. Understand daily balance, control its content and use its strength. That is it. Banks have understood the power of daily balances for years, but few business operators take the time to learn its strength.

Management of these funds is nothing more than making sure that all business-generated revenue streams are effectively controlled and used. To effectively control revenue, business owners must capture maximum dollars for maximum duration. Business owners must fully exploit how these captured dollars are spent. Optimum liquidity results when these ends are reached.

To effectively control and use revenues, business owners must capture maximum dollars for maximum duration.

With optimum liquidity, a business more easily pays bills, expands operations and increases bottom-line profit margins. In a world of fierce competition and rapid corporate failure, small business owners must learn the revenue management techniques found within the

NBP: Turn erratic daily balances into Controlled Daily Balances (CDB).

CDB - Clearing House and Daily Monitoring System

CDB is both a clearing house process and daily monitoring system designed to help businesses generate a bankable cash balance on the corporate books equal to 14% to 18% of the average monthly company revenue stream. This balance should not drop, is apart from existing cash-on-hand and not connected to the corporate account balance at the bank. To control the daily balance of capital is not the same as a hold-back account used by banks and factors to secure lending. CDB is created, controlled and monitored. A hold-back balance takes into account only what exists before cash management - nothing more.

The CDB technique helps businesses generate a corporate bank balance equal to 14% to 18% times the average monthly revenue.

How to Create CDB

Simply stated, a lock-box type account is established to receive all corporate revenue. Monitored daily, a computer-driven, clearing-house process restricts revenue disbursement from this account. A pre-formulated advance rate equal to 1/22nd of each month's estimated revenue stream is systematically transferred to the corporate master account every three days. An average 22 transfers are made each month.

The process continues over again during each ensuing month unless the process is stopped by the owner. Each month, the estimated revenues are updated and the 1/22nd component is recalculated. The idea is to delay the cash flow as long as practical so that the business can take full advantage of the temporary cash by utilizing it as long as possible.

Neither float (checks written, but not processed) nor pre-existing cash-on-hand is a part of CDB.

Business owners become more acutely aware of cash flow and how it works by using CDB techniques. Cash is transferred to the business through a predetermined controlled stream of cash wired to the bank account. The owner manages the money instead of the money managing the owner. Payrolls and vendor expenses are paid in accordance with budgetary goals, not revenue timing.

Negotiations with vendors and suppliers are conducted to push payment arrangements into the next cycle (cycling) where possible and without penalty. Cash is preserved. Good management of cash results in controlled daily balances greater than 15% times monthly revenues. 20% and more is not unheard of. 20% times $1,000,000 monthly revenue stream is $200,000 cash. $200,000 flows to the bottom line as a result of controlling the flow of money, raising awareness of how cash flows and cycling invoices.

More Liquid Operation

Equity does not necessarily increase from CDB usage, but what does most certainly happen is this: Cash seeps up from the depths of the financial statement and sits on the line designated cash, or cash equivalents. The company becomes more liquid. Cash is under control and rises to the top.

Cash seeps up from the depths of the financial statement and sits on the line designated cash, or cash equivalents.

Controlled daily balance arrangements may be ended anytime subject to security/lien arrangements in place. Security liens may come into being when the corporation starts credit lines, receivable factoring or other financial obligations.

CDB Usage

The 15% cash reserve can be used for a variety of purposes: Interest income; to secure a line or letter of credit; to factor the company receivables (novel, but highly creative); to secure real estate or equipment purchases; as a nest egg; or just about any other business spawned usage.

In reality, those who understand the whole notion behind Controlled Daily Balance will turn stagnant assets into cash, increase borrowing levels, provide a new asset base to leverage and increase corporate liquidity. CDB is not credit driven; credit plays no role in the development or approval of the process. Number of years in operation is also immaterial.

Grasp its full meaning and CDB will absolutely force good revenue management.

Buyer's Benefit

Once set up and captured, a buyer, via an escrow closing can figure to bring 90% of Controlled Daily Balance dollars to the closing table as part of the purchase price. A $1,000,000 average monthly revenue stream should bring forward a minimum $135,000. An escrow closing is necessary to accomplish this end, a technique that will be discussed later on.

Chapter Eleven: Holding Company / Virtual Corporation

Today, the antiquated holding company is often called a virtual corporation. A virtual company is created from an original entity whose express purpose is to amplify or enhance that entity, but remains dependent on that entity for its existence. Like a virtual reality machine, where the viewer peers into a world seen as real only by the viewer, a virtual company is real only to the extent that it amplifies or enhances its benefactor, the original entity.

However, as a virtual company grows in personality, significance and momentum, there is always the opportunity to become independent. A salesperson, for example, develops territories and customers under the umbrella of an employer and then may leave to start a new company. As often as not the new company performs better and longer than the one from which it came. The same applies to a virtual corporation.

Remember the lock-box account connected with CDB?

In the instance of Controlled Daily Balance, a virtual corporation is enacted to serve as a processing entity for business revenue. The cash receipts are systematically filtered to the Mother Corporation. How best to use the dollars is also determined. As with any bank, the temporary funds controlled by the virtual corporation are invested to benefit its founder.

A virtual corporation may have many employees. Employment is generally relegated to accounting or other designated central core type functions. Such services, if provided to the original entity, may prove in the long haul to be better managed, more efficient and less costly than when performed by the Mother Corporation.

No Limitations

A virtual corporation might even expand its operation, establish itself as an independent being, or even swell to a more profitable level than its founder. There are no limitations except for those placed on it by the founding entity.

Another example of a virtual corporation is a management company.

Management Company

Management companies are growing in popularity today because of the many advantages that their usage provide. A management company renders another layer of legal protection, furnishes additional leverage potential and represents one more opportunity to expand revenue streams.

Whereas an individual owner is responsible for all aspects of a business operation, a management company forces its participants to concentrate only on the business of management - its only function is to manage. Too often, owners try to do everything. However, it has been shown over and over that no one is good at selling, accounting, management, manufacturing, computer usage, creativity or invention, law, at whatever all at the same time. To manage a business well, a more concentrated effort is required. A management company serves that purpose.

Let us look at another example of a virtual corporation.

Keep Old Corporation

Since some buyers do not want the potential liability associated with the purchase of existing corporate stock, they opt to buy just the assets of the corporation. After closing, the first thing that the seller quickly does is dispose of the original corporation structure.

Some of the sharper buyers on the market, especially those who go after and purchase mid-range businesses, keep the Mother Corporation intact. The reason? The Mother Corporation in many instances is not only well established within its particular market segment, but also has built-in credit potential.

To keep the original corporation intact may bring instant financial wherewithal to the buyer. If structured correctly, the buyer may inherit minimal liability. Here is an example:

A business for sale comes to mind when this concept really made sense. The seller had assets for sale and after closing wanted to shut down his corporation and retire. However, if the seller would agree to keep his corporation intact, the buyer could sell to the 'Mother' Corporation and leverage the receivables created by the transaction. In this way, the seller still maintained a degree of control over the cash flow and insured that any outstanding capital obligations were satisfied. There was no risk to the seller, no obligations, not even extra work. The buyer, in accordance with strict contractual arrangements, would act as a management company over the old corporation.

There was no ownership overlap, no conflict of interest and the whole transaction was at arm's length. Additional leverage was now available, the cost was nominal and when faced with the need for more investor money, which was also not available, here it was - yet another example of how the Natural Business Philosophy works.

Payroll Leasing Company

One of the best illustrations of the virtual corporation is a payroll leasing company. In brief, because it is discussed in a later chapter, a payroll leasing company leases employees to employers. Existing employees of a particular corporation are hired by the payroll leasing firm and leased back. The leasing company invoices the particular corporation for payroll services. A new level of revenue is created.

The Internet has brought about new and exciting uses for the virtual corporation. In the future, more and more individuals will open shop to act as outsourcing agents for past employers and competitors. They will be small businesses working for many others - the ultimate virtual corporation. Corporate costs are expected to drop, productivity is expected to rise and profits will likely increase. The work place will change forever. Individuals will control personal environments, goals and progress - a reversal of today's business community.

Chapter Twelve: Payroll Leasing

Not many small business owners are aware that payroll leasing exists or even what it means. Public companies use payroll leasing plans as do many large private businesses. Payroll leasing is a process whereby a small business may choose to lease its employees from an established payroll leasing company. Current employees are hired and then leased back to the company from which they came. They continue working under the owner's supervision who still makes all operating decisions.

Employee leasing is more than a payroll service. The leasing company becomes the employer of record and is therefore responsible for payroll, payroll taxes, workers' compensation and personnel records. More specific tasks that are handled: Payroll administration, employee personnel records, handbooks, references, workers compensation insurance, unemployment and workers compensation claims, and safety programs.

Payroll administration specifically includes payroll journals, cost reports, tax deposits, quarterly tax returns, annual returns, W-2's and more. Distinct from payroll duties, the cost of insurance may drop due to more employees present in the system of the payroll leasing company; certain tax savings are available; there are no personnel files to keep; and, liability is reduced. The business owner retains the authority to hire, fire and manage the leased employees. Bear in mind, these leased employees were originally employees of the business owner.

In many instances, it costs the business little more to lease its own employees back from a leasing company. If negotiated properly, the owner of the business actually pays no more, little at worst, and takes part in a special cash-saving program with the leasing company. The program is formulated to permit the business to delay 80% of the funding of the payroll for as long as 30 days after it is due.

Employee Leasing Saves Money

To accomplish these savings, the leasing company invoices its client for the full amount of payroll charges, including fees, taxes and any other applicable costs. On a weekly basis, a receivable factoring company advances 80% of the invoice (check local, state and national regulations). 20% is due up front from the client to cover the difference. Four weeks later the first invoice is due and the client company pays the full amount directly to the factoring company. From that amount, 20% (less a fee) is reimbursed to the leasing company and applied to the client's account. Only approved invoices are factored.

What is achieved here is remarkable. For little or no gain in payroll expenses, 80% of the client's payroll dollars each month are saved through a natural delay started by this process. The Natural Business Philosophy, which uses the inherent strengths of a company to help bolster its liquid assets, provides a way to increase cash-on-hand with little or no cost.

If a monthly payroll is say $400,000, 80% ($320,000) is saved as cash-on-hand. To a buyer of this example company, either an escrow closing, or a short-term note to the seller, brings another $320,000 directly to the bottom line.

More Time to Run the Business

Employee leasing is a technique that saves a small company owner time and money, offers employees better benefits than the client company and cuts paperwork. There are no workers' compensation problems, no labor department audits, no insurance claims. Employee leasing saves time, money and headaches; someone else handles administrative duties. It reduces costs - employees are not needed to handle certain office functions. Economy of scale is achieved in payroll administration and employee benefits. The employer is offered the best benefit of all: More time to run the business.

Employee leasing does the payroll, delivers the checks, provides complete payroll reports and makes deposits - federal, state, FICA, employer FICA and unemployment taxes. Employee leasing files all federal and state forms - 941, 940, etc. - and furnishes W2's at the end of the year. It manages claims for unemployment and workers compensation, assures compliance with all state and federal laws and rules, maintains all personnel records and furnishes employee references. Employee leasing reduces liability from employee lawsuits and governmental penalties, provides and administers employee benefits - medical, life, disability, retirement - and provides workers compensation insurance at cost. The risk associated with all payrolls is diminished when another carries out the task.

To repeat, the business owner retains the authority to hire, fire, manage employees and set hours and pay rates. The Natural Business Philosophy works once more.

Buy That Business ... Poor old Daddy didn't Leave you!

Chapter Thirteen: Escrow Closing

Few are aware that an escrow closing is one clever way to close and settle either a merger or an acquisition, whether by outside enterprise or inside management. Many in the business of mergers and acquisitions have never used an escrow closing.

An escrow closing accomplishes several important objectives necessary to more successfully implement a merger or acquisition scenario.

Time to Restructure

First, an escrow closing - merely signing the papers and holding the actual takeover of operations until certain predefined events occur - permits the buyer of an operation to carry out necessary operational restructuring. Perhaps there are going to be specific changes in the way the operation is to be conducted. These changes are best enacted while still operating under existing ownership. It is important to make such arrangements part of the contractual understanding and do an escrow closing as opposed to a wait-and-see attitude after final settlement.

If a business circumstance is to be restructured, or when certain cash prerequisites are pending, an escrow closing allows time to complete these contingencies. While in escrow, there is also the opportunity to become familiar with vendors, or uncover employee problems unimaginable from a distance.

An escrow closing permits a buyer to carry out necessary operational restructuring.

Adjustment Period

Second, there is usually an adjustment period within the organization immediately following a closing when the employees and, particularly management, sometimes the seller, get nervous. It is also during this period that any number of problems, impossible to detect no matter how diligent, come to light. These details might be serious distortions of facts, or simple misunderstandings, but if not addressed might eventually lead the buyer and seller into court. Undisclosed or forgotten payables, an employee's bonus arrangement overlooked, a key employee who all a sudden decides to leave, or an unpaid tax bill might cloud an otherwise uncontaminated closing.

No purchase is flawless. An escrow closing, however, results in the cleansing of many unforeseen, potentially problematic issues before they become legal issues, or create an ever-increasing cloud of suspicion between the seller and buyer.

An escrow closing helps resolve potential problems before they become legal issues.

Stop the Clock

Third, an escrow closing stops the clock. From the time an escrow closing takes place, even though the company is yet officially operated by the seller, corporate revenues and expenses no longer belong to the previous team. All revenues are in essence escrowed - except for what is necessary to operate. These expenses are paid according to a new schedule, maybe one that has been negotiated more favorably by the new team. This doesn't mean that the new team owns the revenue, or controls the expenditures, other than what has been contracted for them to control. What it does mean is that, short of a final closing and settlement, the cash and profits will no longer go to the old. They now, unless otherwise determined, belong to the new.

An escrow closing stops the clock.

Newly created receivables and payables belong to the buyer. So do profits or losses, if any. How does this help the buyer?

Certainly a legal, accounting and budgetary decision, if proper planning has gone into the implementation of a continuing line-of-credit as well as the establishment of adequate working capital, a 30 day escrow closing may permit the buyer to assign accumulated receivables and cash to the seller as part of the purchase price. Cash accumulation refers to CDB reserves, profits and various savings events connected with payroll leasing, inventory handling and other NBP processes.

An escrow closing helps unearth more cash for the buyer to give the seller at closing.

Caution

To restate, cash accumulation during an escrow period is entirely contingent on prudent research by an experienced accountant, attorney and business consultant. There is as much to lose as to gain by improper evaluation of this funding methodology.

For instance, inventory used to create receivables may be adversely affected. Can a buyer survive with a depleted inventory? Perhaps, but can a buyer restore levels of inventory without significantly elevating the payables?

Also, there are going to be irregularities within the revenue stream if existing receivables have been assigned to the seller as part of an escrow event. Can payables be paid, including payroll, during the escrow closing?

To exercise this daring cash gathering technique, extreme caution must be taken to insure that its application will not deplete the operating capital below budgetary standards.

Buy That Business ... Poor old Daddy didn't Leave you!

Chapter Fourteen: The AB Scenario

The Junk Bond Era

In the decade of the 80's, junk bonds symbolized power. Vulnerable companies fell prey to corporate raiders armed with formidable funds collected from the sale of these high yield, high risk securities. Targeted companies were confiscated so that the raiders could squeeze hefty profits from surging stock prices or from the sale of seized assets. Billions of dollars were raised, but the attached debt service proved too much for many once strong business operations.

As one debt-ridden company after another failed to meet interest commitments, the onetime powerful junk bond market lost credibility and sank into oblivion. With its deterioration, the take-over frenzy of the 80's along with its inborn greed ended.

Even though the era of high powered, junk bond financed take-overs is all but forgotten, it is important to understand that mergers and acquisitions are still a strategic, vital component of the business environment. Takeovers can prompt management improvement, expense reductions, profit increases and a more stable financial condition.

But, to acquire another business usually means borrowing capital and the cost can be prohibitive, especially to the small business owner. Small business owners can seldom look to Wall Street for financial assistance; they must rely on more conventional sources for funding: Banks and comparable financial institutions.

Hesitant to lend to less than perfect borrowers and soured by the junk bond fiasco in the 80's, lenders now choose more conservative avenues in which to place depositor's cash. Thus, expansion money - so important to small businesses - is often scarce.

So, when funding is limited, how does an ambitious, small business operator expand? There is an answer and it is a good one!

In early 1991, I founded a growth process that not only created horizontal expansion; it produced vertical growth while at the same time it cut expenses. I called this procedure the "AB Scenario." A financial windfall! What makes it different from conventional financing?

Money! This practice can be performed with little or none of it. The AB Scenario has the purchasing power of the junk bond without the associated debt service. And, the methodology places the most conservative business operator at ease.

In Brief, What is the AB Scenario?

In general, the AB Scenario is a means by which small business operations can effectively merge with and/or acquire other business operations through a joint venture arrangement. Opposite from vertical development - growth of product sales - this growth is termed horizontal or enhancement through the merger/acquisition of another.

Horizontal expansion or acquisition of another entity can double or even triple a company's gross revenues. By comparison, vertical expansion or the increase of revenues through greater sales adds only about 10 to 15% per year. The AB Scenario is the ultimate outsourcing vehicle.

The AB Scenario is a methodology which requires little or no cash, can be performed repeatedly as if empire building; it takes full advantage of available resources. The transaction also requires minimum legal input, allows personnel to best use personal skills and generally allows one company or the other to maintain control of the operation without argument.

Four Obstacles to Overcome: Finding a dynamic, business-literate management team; convincing a potential joint venture candidate that the AB Scenario would cause him to lose both his personal identity and all that he had worked for over his lifetime (protected by enforceable legal contracts); convincing a potential joint venture candidate that if he decided not to participate in the AB Scenario, others might absorb the best acquisitions first (too may categories of business to be logical); and, finding only those joint venture candidates whose acquisition cost does not exceed 3 to 10 X net income before taxes and profits, excluding real estate and particular assets.

Although there is little to limit the parties from agreeing to whatever works for the majority, there are several elements that must be considered as part of the formation of Company C.

1. When Company A locates several possible Company B's, negotiations between the candidates should include the resolution of specific monetary issues that will surely cause strife if left unresolved. For example, the previous existing 12 months operating profits, important to any Company B candidate, should be contractually locked and guaranteed to that candidate, at least, for the first 12 months of operations under Company C.

2. Personnel strengths must be evaluated, and employees, even management, should be positioned where best suited. Although employee manipulation for the good of Company C sounds like a good idea, this area of negotiation has to be handled with great care and finesse.

3. One very reliable reason to participate in the AB Scenario is to save money. Duplicated efforts can be eliminated and operating expenses

reduced. Accounting, legal and insurance functions determined duplications of effort can be eliminated where possible. Other expense areas, such as cost of space, utilities, and telephone, can be reduced when it is proven frugal to do so.

4.   Inspect all debt, old and new, and renegotiate the terms and conditions.   Old debt, especially, can sometimes be reduced, sometimes eliminated.

5.   New and more sophisticated sales and marketing programs are possible to instigate under a new umbrella. There is now more buying power, more manpower and more incentives to produce a more effective marketing program. Combined, the two entities have more ideas, better experience levels, and a higher level of motivation.

6.   At some point, say one year after closing and settlement, the one coming into the merger - Company B - is permitted to exit without penalty. In fact, Company B's original corporation can be left intact for that very purpose, and Company C can pay those expenses.

AB Scenario Options

Company A instigates a joint venture arrangement with a designated company B and together form a new company C. Company A may elect to provide central core functions (functions related to services provided to company C such as accounting, sales, banking, management, efficiency, product assistance, business consultation, expansion and growth, restructuring, budget, etc.); and, *company B might choose to handle the fundamental business operations.* Company C becomes the actual operating entity.

One ownership strategy is for Co. A to *own 51% of company C.* One big risk to company A under the described circumstance is the possibility that company B could take everything for itself since company B is in control of the operation.

A major risk to company B is that company A could take all new business - which in time might mean all the business. Company A owns controlling interest.

Potential candidates for Company B might be: Vendors, suppliers, sub-trade members, the competition, business associates, business customers, owners of similar businesses, businesses whose functions add central core support such as accounting, etc.

Potential Snags

Potential candidates to be considered for a merger/acquisition scenario may suffer from one or more operational predicaments. Be aware of what these problems can be; put forth a reasonable effort to uncover them; and, analyze what effect the problems found will have on Company C. A brief list is: Poor management, undercapitalized, moral problems, company stripped of money and assets by owner, bad reputation, passé management attitude, poor or no corporate credit, poor or slow paying receivables, heavy debt load, payables out of proportion to receivables, cash flow behind accrual, too many employees, no budget, no business plan, accounting reporting outdated or incomprehensible, inappropriate product line, profit margin too small, stiff competition, out of control overhead, extensive management and owner perks, sales down, bankrupt financials, incomplete financial statements, generally accepted accounting ratios not to standard, etc.

The Meeting

After exhausting personal acquaintances, make cold calls to selected businesses in the local area. The calls should be made by someone who possesses good phone skills, perhaps a personal secretary willing to be trained.

Talk only to the owner, or a secretary who has the authority to set appointments for the owner. The idea is to set a personal meeting to discuss the possibility of a joint venture. No other details over the phone! Using a secretary to call in lieu of one in charge of company A eliminates questions best answered in person.

Preparation for the meetings is relatively easy. The topic is joint venture. A joint venture means what it says: A business arrangement between two or more parties whereby each intends to profit. Draw a triangle on a piece of paper showing company A (you), company B (them) and company C (A + B). Simple!

Some basic reasons to say Yes: Vertical expansion, networking, sales training, marketing program, crossover networking, overhead decreases, operational efficiency, automatic revenue Increases, free to do only what is enjoyable, financial Assistance, elimination of duplicated efforts, 12 Month Guarantee, central core functions, no loss of earned benefits from giving up the operation of Company B, original company remains, if necessary.

After the first, brief presentation, determine the interest level of the candidate. From leading questions, learn whether the candidate is interested or simply curious. Don't waste time; find out the level of interest. Ask the candidate: Yes, or No? Close the deal, or thank the candidate for coming.

Chapter Fifteen: Expense Cuts

As a business owner builds an operation, decisions are made that sometimes prove to be beneficial, other times, ineffectual. When a judgment is made that eventually proves to be harmful to the business, what happens when that decision is irreversible? For example, what might be the result if long-time family members or members of management become sluggish?

Family First

Friendship associated with family members influences an owner's judgment when faced with the need to reduce wages, benefits, or jobs. What once may have been a great idea to hire Uncle Joe to fill the position of sales manager, when his performance confirms otherwise, how do you fire a relative? Even if the future survival of the company is in the hands of Uncle Joe, due to kinship, the owner may be unable to replace him.

Correspondingly, in instances where a known family member is given what is perceived as special treatment - better wages or benefits - fellow employees may feel hurt, or worse, bitter. Bitterness in the work place lowers productivity. Operational effectiveness suffers; so do profits. Opportunities are missed.

The financial consequences associated with family members of the owner who no longer benefit the company, are more advantageously dealt with by the buyer.

Long-time Employees

Long-time management might be a problem, too. The same routine over and over easily dulls the senses. Without some sort of motivation, managers are subject to boredom. If a feeling of job security develops over time. That comfort level lessens job effectiveness. Convention rules the work place contrary to innovation.

The financial consequences associated with members of management who have become apathetic are more advantageously dealt with by the buyer.

Expenses

Expense reductions may be impossible under these circumstances and the owner who accepts the finality of the situation must then live with it. A new owner, however, does not have to stay with protocol. Modifications to personnel, management and employee duties, as well as general operational expenditures, are definite options to the buyer. Not to take advantage of an opportunity to affect business profits sanctions apathy. A new owner should act instantly; there is no better time than post-closing. In some instances, much is accomplished even before settlement.

However, there are times in the year when such adjustments are not in the best interest of the company. These times are usually when business is sluggish, such as construction starts during the winter months. Making modifications then might damage moral, place the operation in harm's way, or just drive the business out of business. Timing is important.

Nonetheless, lost profitability is readily retrieved and cash-on-hand markedly increased once cost savings measures are carried out.

The prime target periods to trim expenses including those costs pertinent to personnel are during an escrow closing and the first month post-closing.

Goals

When new blood takes part in the management or ownership of an operation, the common goal to shoot for is a 5% minimum expense reduction. Supposing the expenses total for an average month is $200,000, a reduction of $10,000 is certainly reasonable. 5% should not impair the operation, unless the operation is in financial trouble, or has already been cut to the bone by an owner who bled the company. In either case, the buyer should walk away from the company anyway.

Shoot for a minimum expense reduction of 5%.

The Math

$10,000 makes a lot of difference to new management or ownership. It may help offset debt service, buy needed equipment or supplies, provide incentives for management to drive the business upward, and as it accumulates, improve the financial statement. $10,000 may not seem all that much immediately, but if left untouched for 12 months, $10,000 monthly grows to six figures not counting interest.

A buyer who is able to justify even greater expense reductions can really increase cash-on-hand dollars post-closing. If the monthly payroll is $200,000, a 10% manpower reduction immediately places $20,000 in the bank. Dependent on what the cash requirements are to close, $20,000 definitely helps the buyer.

Overall Expense Cuts

Argue that a company pays out every penny it receives for expenses and the truth is probably not far away. A business that brings in an average of $1,000,000 each month might pay out as much as $1,000,000 in wages, materials, taxes and so on. A minimum 5% saved equates to $50,000, not once, but each month on the average. $50,000 is generated in theory within 30 days. Over 12 months, the number grows to $600,000. $600,000 is a lot of cash saved! A buyer may forecast 60% times an average month's revenue stream in new cash.

In 12 months, a 5% monthly expense cut equates to as much as 60% times an average month's revenue in rescued cash.

Chapter Sixteen: Brokerage Commissions

When a business broker sells a business, a commission is due. The owner of the business sold must pay the fee at closing as part of closing costs. Commission schedules are usually calculated in accordance with the "Lehman Scale." On the first $1,000,000 of the selling price obtained by the broker, 5% is due; 4% of the next $1,000,000; 3% of the next $1,000,000; 2% of the next $1,000,000; and, 1% of any funds realized thereafter. A sale that generates a $5,000,000 selling price entitles the broker to $50,000 plus $40,000 plus $30,000 plus $20,000 plus $10,000, or $150,000.

If payables and debt service are assumed by the buyer, the dollar amount of each is added to the final selling price. In the above example, if the combined payable and debt assumption were $3,000,000, the commission is calculated on $8,000,000.

Some brokers use a "double" Lehman scale. In other words, the amount charged is twice the norm. In the example given, the commission due at closing is $360,000. Commission arrangements are decided up front and put in writing to protect both the owner and the broker.

Commission Delay

A shrewd buyer might be able to negotiate a compromise with the broker whereby the broker agrees to either delay the payment of commission until sometime after closing, give a share of the commission to the buyer, or take part in the ownership of the business. The buyer at settlement deducts the dollar amount of any such negotiated transaction from the cash requirement due the seller. Prior to any delayed payment agreement, the means to eventually pay the debt must be planned.

Since the seller pays the full amount regardless of the buyer's dealings with the broker, if 100% of the aforementioned $360,000 is delayed until after closing, the buyer gains $360,000 in cash toward the purchase price. The delay gives the buyer time to generate capital from the business to pay the debt.

$360,000, if split, gives the buyer $180,000 to work with. In some states, sharing fees requires that the buyer be licensed as either a real estate broker, or a business broker, or both.

Ownership by the broker, if not deemed a conflict of interest, grants the buyer whatever value is negotiated. The value is deducted from what is owed the seller at closing. In regard to sharing in corporate ownership, the broker must feel confident that over the long haul, more money will be realized than by taking the commission

Since a business broker usually represents the seller, to work with the buyer other than as a go-between may be a conflict of interest. Barring a conflict, to consider any kind of split with a buyer the broker must first gain confidence in the buyer. Will the delayed commission be paid on time? That is the number one concern.

A judgment note, or a percentage of temporary ownership might be offered the broker as collateral. Should that be unsatisfactory, without other buyers, the broker may cooperate anyway. What are his or her options?

Chapter Seventeen: Outsiders Have 20/20 Vision

Not long ago, a business person devised a theory that went something like this:

If a certain company A purchases a certain company B, and company B purchases a certain company C, and company C turns around and purchases company A, a single company is created. Each of the three companies is assumed to be similar in financial strength and the terms that collectively close such a deal are assumed adequate by the existing stockholders. At closing, each company's stockholders receive whatever is negotiated and turn over ownership to whoever negotiated the buyout. The buyer may be management, existing minority stockholders, or neither.

Because of the theory circumstances, there may be no need for outside investment money and probably no personal credit. If a management team had designed this merger, it might very well implement the transaction without cash, credit and outside help. The closing might take place inside the offices of three businesses without so much as one cent of outside input, influence, or interference.

In theory, what has happened here is this: A deal has been structured within the confines of the Natural Business Philosophy. For those who grasp the principles derived from this hypothetical merger/acquisition example, the concept is commonplace. To corporate insiders, the notion is also easy to comprehend, yet worthless without innate creativity and an understanding of the full import of the NBP.

There is no reason why three companies cannot be merged into one large unit without personal capital or credit. The assets of each business are used to collateralize any borrowings deemed necessary to swing the financing. Existing stockholders receive all required funds and notes to give up stock ownership. Together, the three management teams are no doubt the best qualified to run the connected operations. Elementary logic. Insiders benefit if they are smart enough to take advantage of the situation, or smart enough to design the actual scenario.

But, why do so many members of the business community, especially the small business environment, fail to grasp what the ABC example demonstrates?

No Forest for the Trees

Insiders - e.g., management - are usually the last to see the forest for the trees. They are often too deeply entrenched in daily work chores to see anything other than what is near at hand. Furthermore, more often than not, management will not consider taking on more responsibilities even though it is generally management who is accountable one way or the other for all responsibilities. An acquisition as mentioned is out of the question.

Experience has taught me that this same group believes that not only does it lack the collective financial capacity to take over total company ownership, it does not possess sufficient expertise to run the whole show. No one would know this from listening to conversations among one another though. Each has an opinion as to the other's talents and shortcomings.

Ironically, it is usually the management team that is responsible for the success or failure of any given business and without this expertise, experience and dedication, most companies would not survive long. But to put themselves in a position of absolute authority and responsibility is the most terrifying thought in most of their minds. Forget the fact that they are in that position anyway; they just do not want to admit it, recognize it, or be it.

So, insiders are usually the last to take advantage of a purchase situation, even if an acquisition is possible. I have seen this plight over and over again. It usually takes an outsider to see the forest for the trees, one who is not afraid to take realistic chances.

Many take-overs have been put together by individuals who are far less qualified that those over whom they take.

What is learned?

What is learned from this study is that within any company - deemed suitable by the Natural Business Philosophy - are valuable, often hidden assets. If the assets are identified and manipulated accurately, they provide major deductions from the selling price. Acquisitions might very well take place without one cent of cash, credit, or outside input, influence and interference.

Not having to borrow more money, or get costly, outside investment dollars, helps keep debt service under control - part of the Natural Business Philosophy.

Outsiders have 20/20 Vision if they know the Natural Business Philosophy.

Buy That Business … Poor old Daddy didn't Leave you!

Chapter Eighteen: Pre-selling Assets

Selected assets might be pre-sold to help generate capital to close an acquisition, or working capital after closing. To determine what assets to sell, the buyer must analyze the equipment list along with associated appraisals. From this examination, a determination is made as to what pieces of equipment are unnecessary to the operation and what items might be sold and replaced by a comparable piece of leased equipment.

Pre-sell the selections subject to closing. Hand-in-hand with a leaseback contract (discussed later), cash is generated from selling, or leasing back assets. Which road to take depends on which avenue offers the most dollars? Only a portion of the value is gained via a leaseback, but 100% of the value is gained through a sale. However, in some instances, a sale is impractical due to distressed local market conditions. A leaseback may then be the more profitable course to take.

Selected assets may be pre-sold to help generate capital to close an acquisition, or working capital after closing.

Split Business

Some business operations lend themselves to splitting into two distinct units. For instance, say a manufacturer of cabinetry also sells its products retail. To split the company into a sales organization and a manufacturing operation makes economic sense. If split, there may be a ready market to sell off either the manufacturing end, or the sales unit.

When the split is made at arm's length (the same people do not own both entities), any dealings between the two organizations become real in that invoices sent between them may be sold for cash. New cash flow levels automatically become a byproduct. Any benefits derived by doing business between the separate businesses after closing are obviously encouraged and kept intact.

Something else. Often a better run operation is created by splitting an organization into two. Each entity is managed more effectively because the management concentrates on either one business or the other.

Value is another consideration. The two entities separated may be worth more than when each was combined. Before closing, one or the other may be pre-sold to help fund the purchase of the combined operation.

Two Entities in Place

In other cases, a company is already two separate entities and both are for sale as one. Usually this type of business is owned by the same person and is therefore not classified at arm's length. However if one entity or the other is sold, a new owner/buyer enters the picture. The transaction is now at arm's length and right away the two businesses might choose to deal between each other to generate valid receivables. The dealing is real and each may sell the invoices issued to the other. The doing creates value and value influences cash flow.

Say, for example, Company AB, a manufacturing and sales organization grosses $6,000,000 annually, but individually the manufacturing end grosses $3,000,000 and the sales end grosses $6,000,000. Since the transaction is not at arm's length, any sales between the two entities are considered in-house. Instead of $9,000,000 annual revenue, the reported gross is only $6,000,000.

Still and all, if an outsider buys the manufacturing end, the annual gross sales are recorded as $9,000,000 and all transactions with the sales end are then at arm's length. There are exceptions to what happens here, but normally this is what occurs when an outsider buys part of a company. To better grasp the concept, imagine that one person never owned the two entities.

$9,000,000 annual sales mean greater CDB, more receivables to sell and better management in place.

Buy That Business ... Poor old Daddy didn't Leave you!

Chapter Nineteen: Stock Sale to Management and Seller

There are many management people who would like to have a portion of ownership in the corporation for which they work, but do not know how to get it. A buyer may provide the perfect passage. Sellers are usually comfortable with their management members; selling corporate ownership to them is certainly acceptable. Even if some members of the team do not have cash to pay for the stock, a short-term note to the seller is satisfactory. So, if a buyer can persuade management personnel to act in partnership, even a short-term note to the seller reduces the capital requirement at closing.

If the team ends agreeing to buy 20% of the corporation's stock, and the seller is willing to accept payment for the stock by way of a note, the buyer's share of stock to purchase is reduced accordingly. To give up 20%, even double that, is not going to hinder a buyer's ability to control an acquisition. In reality, it should help; more heads.

The note can be paid by way of payroll deduction, or in cash installments. With a track history, sometimes only one or two months, the collective notes might be sold to a note broker for cash. The note, to be marketable, will need to be discounted. The cost to discount the note may be worth it to the seller who is looking for as much cash as possible, and to the buyer who is trying to come up with as little cash as possible.

A $1,000,000 sales price offset by management's 20% participation drops the buyer's capital burden by $200,000. If a note broker finds these particular notes attractive, an offer of perhaps 80% (90% tops) will be tendered. The question then becomes; will the seller accept the discount to receive immediate cash in lieu of a short-term note? The seller will consider the cash lost through the discount versus the value of cash-in-hand. Most sellers will choose the latter.

From this example, notice that there is no need for a buyer to purchase 100% of the corporate stock. Since 51% is really all that is necessary to retain control of a corporation, management's participation in the ownership of the company does not intimidate the buyer; in fact, it makes good business sense.

On the other hand, the seller may be persuaded to hold a portion of the company's stock, too. To retain some ownership is often a good move by the seller, especially if the buyer comes off as a confident, trustworthy administrator who most likely will influence the future growth and financial stability of the operation. Seller input is minimal, but the potential of profits looms and that in itself is a viable reason to retain stock.

Whether it is the management personnel, or the seller, or both, ownership offers all shareholders an incentive to work harder, take the operation more seriously and strive to make the company financially strong and profitable. Sounds like a win-win scenario.

Cash Advantages

To review, when the purchase price is reduced even 20%, the cash requirement most definitely will fall. If the purchase price is $1,000,000 and 50% - or $500,000 - is paid in cash, a 20% stock sale by others reduces the buyer's cash requirement by $100,000.

Sell more stock; come up with less cash.

Chapter Twenty: Inventory Handling

A revolving line-of-credit often includes cash advances against a company's acceptable inventory. Acceptable inventory includes raw materials and finished goods, but usually does not include materials that are obsolete, specialized, or not yet completed. Lenders normally like to include the receivables as part of the financial package when advancing against the inventory. Sound banking reason prescribes that all cash flow is directed into bank tills. The line-of-credit then revolves continuously and advances given are only against new receivables and fresh inventory.

Dependent on the type of inventory, the advance rate is as low as 30% of cost and as high as 60%. Gold bars may bring more, but usually the rate averages about 50%.

Lenders are concerned they will not be paid, so when considering whether to advance money against a particular inventory, they must be comfortable knowing that the goods can be sold at will if the borrower defaults. Business owners get rid of inventory to raise cash and in some instances, the bank is not reimbursed. Since there is plenty of room for internal manipulation by an owner, banks are unusually cautious when advancing money against inventory.

When neither the company nor the buyer can get a bank line-of-credit, but a large portion of the company's assets are inventory related, what can be done to leverage the inventory using the NBP?

Inventory Leverage

One way to leverage the inventory is to return it. Yes, return it. Send it back and then re-buy what is necessary. In most instances, a company heavy in inventory needs to make cuts anyway.

One way to leverage inventory is to send it back and then re-buy what is necessary.

Returned inventory means that the payables owed for that particular inventory are no longer due. Cash is thus saved. Further, if inventory is returned and re-bought, a new payable is generated by the supplier. The payment date is delayed and more cash is saved. Many bright buyers raise large amounts of cash in this manner. The cost to return merchandise and the effect on the business must be considered before returning inventory. However, if performed prudently, this proven cash saving methodology uncovers money the natural way.

For example, if the potential inventory return dollar is $100,000, less any associated costs, whatever is due during the month when the goods are returned stays in the bank. $100,000 is a lot of working capital to keep on the table through an act as simple as sending back inventory.

There is generally no need for massive inventory stockpiles. Some companies have inventory delivered on a need-to-have basis. Only those goods needed that moment are required. Other companies cannot survive under this methodology. The gist here, however, is that most inventory levels can be cut.

Chapter Five tells the story of a real company that had an overabundance of inventory on-hand. When measured by an unbiased outsider, the overage was substantial. A conservative inventory dollar to return for credit was $500,000. No argument; it should have been done a long time ago.

The credit meant that a $500,000 cash savings occurred after relevant payables were credited. These dollars did not have to be recommitted. In addition, it was agreed that overstocked goods in the amount of $400,000 were to be returned and repurchased later. $900,000 altogether.

Chapter Twenty-One: Notes

Notes represent a little known source of immediate cash. Notes, sometimes called cash flows, income streams, or paper, are simply debt instruments. They provide cash flows to the owner of the note and are usually secured by an asset that is captured if the payments are not made.

The most common type of notes are real estate mortgages, trust deeds, lottery winnings, structured settlements, annuities, royalties, leases, insurance benefits, retirement accounts, credit cards and home improvement paper. Some notes are secured and some are not. Notes are everywhere and somewhere there is an investor willing to pay cash for it.

Several years ago, a colleague designed a noteworthy of attention. The business he founded, sold individual home alarm systems that triggered when fire broke out on the premises, or if a criminal broke into the premises. Either the police or the fire department was notified if a fire or break-in occurred. Each tenant signed a 36 month monitoring contract. The alarm was connected to a central monitoring desk which constantly watched for any interruption in the system.

Since many businesses offered systems similar to the one my associate sold, the cost had to be competitive. Consequently, the cost of his alarm was close to the sales price. Profits were slim. Larger operations thrived; smaller businesses offering the same service struggled. What to do?

After some deliberation, common sense dictated that to cut costs it would be necessary to sell a whole bunch of alarm systems. But, how? An idea came. Why not approach management of a multi-unit building and try to sell an alarm system for each unit? As one apartment building has many residents, dozens of alarm systems could be sold to just one customer. The idea was certainly a better plan than going door-to-door in the spread-out suburbs. The notion sounded reasonable so several local apartment managers and owners were asked to listen to a sales presentation. An incentive program was put together to entice the sale. Simply stated, the inducement gave participants an opportunity to share in the profits.

When all was said and done, the notion made it possible to reduce costs, thus increase profits. However, that is not the best part of this story.

There are several, national alarm-monitoring companies in the United States. Individual alarm systems, when triggered by fire or break-in, send an electronic message to these companies. After investigation, the operator on duty reports the incident directly to the proper local authority and immediately, appropriate action is taken. A fire truck or police car is dispatched.

Whereas monitoring companies are a growth industry, they seek to purchase monitoring contracts created by smaller alarm sales operations. My colleague offered to sell his monitoring contracts (notes) to one of them. Instead of waiting years to get back project costs, the monitoring company was willing to pay him a generous portion of expected receipts up front.

The amount tendered by the monitoring companies was much greater than the cost of the system and more profit was assured. The gain was more than what could be made by installing the units in single residences and performing the monitoring task locally. Self-generated by creativity, this note arrangement was ingenious. Some notes are not as clever; business notes for example.

Notes privately produced, when an owner sells a property or business, are frequently sold to a note broker. These notes are normally sold at a discount. In other words, when the paper is transferred, the buyer pays less than face value. A $100,000 instrument may sell for $88,000 - a 12% discount. Without a discount, what is the motivation for a private investor to purchase the note?

Small business notes range from $50,000 to $150,000, or more. A buyer of a business operation may be able to sell a solid, well-negotiated note held by the seller. Look for these opportunities. Discuss the discount and determine whether the discount is going to affect the note sale.

Cash is more important to most sellers than paper.

Buy That Business ... Poor old Daddy didn't Leave you!

Chapter Twenty-Two: Equipment Leaseback

If a buyer decides to sell selected pieces of equipment presently used in the business to either help with closing costs, or to operate the business after settlement, the equipment either sells, or it does not. Whether it is free-and-clear, or liened, office equipment, heavy equipment, shop, plant, or manufacturing machinery may be sold. The buyer gets cash if it sells, but what if the equipment does not sell? Consider a leaseback arrangement.

One way, although oftentimes costly, is to set up a leaseback contract. What is a leaseback contract? Qualified company equipment is sold to a leasing firm at near market value and then leased back to the company. An appraisal of the equipment is sought and based on that appraisal, an equipment lender simply buys the equipment from the business, pays the business an agreed on sum of money, and leases the equipment back to the operation. If the money offered for the equipment is sufficient to warrant an agreement, the buyer has access to another source of funding.

Some instances require no appraisal, financials or even tax returns

Equity is turned into cash without going to the market to sell the equipment. No waiting for an offer; no need to advertise and haggle.

There is no specific rule as to how much a lender will pay for used equipment, but whatever the market value is, the lender will pay as much as practical. Say a business owns free-and-clear equipment, trucks for example, valued at $500,000. Many lenders will pay as much as 90% of that value, or $450,000. Some will pay much less; 80% is the norm. In some instances, when there is an existing lien against the equipment, there may still be sufficient equity to pursue a leaseback arrangement. At least some cash might be gained from the transaction.

Equipment is leased for up to five years, with an option to buy it back at the end of the term for as little as $1.00. The equipment stays in place without interruption.

Specialized equipment is usually not subject to leaseback contracts.

The value of the equipment as well as any associated debt come off the balance sheet; the monthly lease payments are part of the income statement.

Before contracting to do a leaseback, the mathematics and what a lease means to the operation must make good business sense. Expenses are closing costs and interest rates. Some interest rates are as high as 24% per year. Closing costs are usually minimal. Further, in a leaseback contract, the business no longer owns the equipment, and if in default, stands to lose it. Of course, even if the business owns the equipment, default brings about the same result.

Chapter Twenty-Three: Capitalize and Renegotiate Debt

Capitalize Debt

To capitalize debt means to convert existing principal owed by the business to ownership in the company. Debt is exchanged for stock. The changeover lowers long-term debt and consequently increases stockholder equity. As debt decreases, equity rises. Sometimes this modest action turns negative stockholder equity into a positive number which in turn might prod the corporate bank to increase credit lines.

To capitalize debt means to convert existing principal owed by the business to ownership in the company.

A typical bank or long-term lender usually will not be interested in converting its debt into ownership. However, private lenders owed money by the company may entertain such a notion; so might passive partners. Vendors and suppliers are also good candidates for debt capitalization.

Say a vendor is owed $100,000 for inventory delivered and the payment is due in 30 days. In simple terms, if that payment is delayed for another 30 days, $100,000 cash falls to the bottom line. The money is not spent, so it will sit unless the owner is in financial difficulty, or the owner spends the found money on personal assets.

Buyers particularly benefit from debt capitalization, not only from a cash standpoint, but also from the positive effect it has on corporate financial statements. There is no need to save the cash, however, if the buyer proves to be imprudent, lack the essentials of budgets, or is just plain foolish. In the end, the cash saved will be wasted.

If debt capitalization is impractical, or perhaps insufficient to dent the money requirements, try to at least renegotiate some of the terms and conditions of the debt.

Never give up.

Re-negotiate Debt

Like capitalizing debt, where debt is converted into ownership in the company, re-negotiating debt offers new opportunities to reduce principal and monthly principal and interest payments. Both instances - debt capitalization and debt re-negotiation - bring about an enhancement of any corporation's financial position. Potential individual or institutional candidates for debt re-negotiation must first be identified; then, the buyer must decide how to approach them.

To re-negotiate debt is a smart business move, unless the owner has robbed the business of its cash flow. A wise buyer always looks for an opportunity to extend payment terms. To save cash is the goal. Cash savings contribute to the cash requirements at closing and settlement.

Bank loans are more difficult to restructure. There is hope though, if the renewal of terms enables the bank to end with a better deal. The bank may re-negotiate, if in the end, interest rates are elevated, principal payments are accelerated, or greater collateral is given. The cost of such action must support the act. When the cost to reduce a bank loan is greater than the long-term benefit, there is plainly no need to make changes.

Equipment Refinancing

Refinancing equipment works to the buyer's advantage, too. To get equity from equipment, it is necessary to either sell the unit, or refinance it. Refinancing is prefaced on equity - the difference between what the apparatus is worth on the market and the value of any liens in place. Cash is squeezed from the asset as a result of refinancing ... subject to the amount of equity present.

Since selling a particular piece of equipment may sometimes be difficult under the time constraints imposed by a pending closing, it often proves wiser to refinance the piece.

Buy That Business ... Poor old Daddy didn't Leave you!

Chapter Twenty-Four: Partners, PCG, and Real Estate

Partner Company or Joint Venture Partner

To combine one potential acquisition candidate with another potential candidate may be the only way to close a deal. For instance, if a particular company sells cabinetry, and another company provides the hardware, if the transaction makes financial sense, try to include both in the purchase package. The second company may serve as partner to the buyer to add financial strength to the purchase transaction, or its owner may choose to sell the company to the buyer per an option arrangement.

To combine one potential acquisition candidate with another potential candidate may be the only way to close a deal.

One company or the other may have assets to trade across the table. Expenses are reduced when duplicate central core functions (accounting, sales and marketing, manufacturing, management, etc.) are eliminated after closing. There might also be a cash advantage gained by selling products or services between the two. With more levels of revenue, leverage increases. Increased leverage brings more cash opportunities.

For example, a recent multiple acquisition provides insight into how two operations leverage off each other. One company operated trucks up and down the East Coast of the United States; the other sold wholesale building products in and around a major eastern city. Each owned trucks; both employed drivers and equipment personnel.

The trucks from the builder supply company were sold to the trucking company and leased back. As a result of that transaction, the supply company's equity grew; more was paid for the trucks than what showed as book value on its balance sheet. The trucking company took over vehicle maintenance for the supply company and was paid the money that normally went to an outside contractor for the same service. Since the trucking company was in the business of maintenance, it was able to provide the service at a profit.

Since its manager was a CPA, the supply company profitably performed certain accounting functions for the trucking company. Besides outsourcing, there were some asset advantages. Several trucks went from one company to the other and some equipment changed hands as well. Each endeavor was designed to produce a gain.

The closings took place on one day, the supply company in the afternoon and the trucking company at night. Without outsourcing and asset trades, the closing table would undoubtedly have been more difficult to reach. All in all, the transaction went smoothly. In time, each operation adjusted to the crossover ideology. An arm's length transaction is vital in such dealings.

In addition to outsourcing and asset trades, an outside investor, perhaps an associate, may likewise be induced to enter into a multiple purchase agreement. The terms may be permanent, or temporary. Collateral and a buyer's credibility are critical to whether an outside investor decides to join. A joint venture partner's capital, or credit, or company may be what is necessary to complete a multiple acquisition. PCG

PCG stands for Private Capital Group. Using the processes found in this writing, it is possible, even wise, to put together a group of companies that will serve as a Private Capital Group. A PCG raises sufficient capital to do just about any deal that makes sense to all the parties.

No one in the group has to actually put up money at the start. The NBP provides the means to generate capital for each of the participants. Once in place, there is no need to put the funds into an escrow account; only express a desire to forward the funds should an agreeable acquisition be found.

A PCG adds monetary strength to any buyer's wherewithal because the processes found within the NBP have been multiplied over a group of buyers, not a single buyer. More cash is available and more management potential exists. Automatically, the number of opportunities to consider grows.

A gang of ten companies means investment capital in the millions, all gained from the processes found in the Natural Business Philosophy. For example, if each of the ten companies exhibits monthly revenues of $1,000,000, the Average Daily Balance program likely collects $1,500,000. $1,500,000 is obtained after using only one NBP program.

Add to CDB what might be leveraged from a potential acquisition candidate and the dollar amount expands even further. Another $1,500,000 from a candidate - $3,000,000 total - means that a company costing twice that much - $6,000,000 - might be purchased without additional funding. Add an additional $1,000,000 to the pot and the purchase price capacity rises to $8,000,000.

When the $1,500,000 CDB figure is supplemented by another NBP program, say payroll leasing - potentially at no cost to the user - an additional $2,500,000 should come to the table (25% minimum payroll expenses X $1,000,000 X 10). Now the purchase price potential rises to $10,000,000 ($1,500,000 + $2,500,000 + $1,000,000 X 2). Readers who are beginning to get the gist of the PCG concept might think that $10,000,000 is conservative. Perhaps it is!

Consider this. Remember those example businesses for sale in Chapter Six? Instead of trying to buy one of those businesses, ask each company to join together and form a Private Capital Group. The goal is to locate and purchase a company with the financial wherewithal equal to or greater than the combined size and strength of its members. A review of the businesses listed in Chapter Six shows that the following ten companies might make good candidates for a PCG:

Ten Example Companies to Consider for a PCG

1. A commercial roofing company with sales of $8,800,000 and adjusted earnings of $740,000.

2. A design/build commercial contractor with sales of $40,000,000 and adjusted earnings of $750,000.

3. A manufacturer/distributor of interior window coverings with sales of $4,574.000 and adjusted earnings of $528,000.

4. Manufacturer and distributor of propellants and explosives with sales of $10,000,000 and adjusted earnings of $1,000,000.

5. Sportswear manufacturing company with sales of $11,300,000 and adjusted earnings of $1,500,000.

6. Specialty trucking firm with sales of $10,000,000 and adjusted earnings of $2,000,000.

7. Ranch, feed and equestrian supply with sales of $4,835,000 and adjusted earnings of $251,000.

8. Wholesale beverage distributor with sales of $16,658,000 and adjusted earnings of $1,055,000.

9. Medical professional placement agency with sales of $6,960,000 and adjusted earnings of $345,000.

10. National interior design firm with sales of $6,500,000 and adjusted earnings of $725,000.

Add the annual revenues of the ten businesses together and divide by 12. The average monthly income stream is about $10,000,000. A Controlled Daily Balance account should yield $1,500,000 at no cost. Contingent on the corporate credit of individual members of the PCG, likely $2,000,000 cash savings drops to the CDB account when PCG members switch to an Employee Lease Back program. The cost here may also be zero if discounts are taken for early payments.

$5,000,000 is in the till, maybe without any cost to the user, and the potential acquisition company has not yet been tapped. The advantage of a Private Capital Group should become immediately evident to readers. Imagine how much funding might be raised with more inventiveness.

For those bold enough to seek out companies to take part in a PCG, the number of purchase opportunities is intensely enhanced. Without the financial strength brought about by additional corporate entities, a lone buyer must choose potential candidates that match narrow guidelines.

With the backing of a PCG, a buyer picks possibilities based on aspirations, not narrow guidelines.

Obviously, there is a need to bring expert legal and accounting expertise aboard whenever in quest of an acquisition. When the buyer is a Private Capital Group, the necessity for legal and accounting ingenuity is even more apparent.

Real Estate

Real Estate is one asset that most banks and other lenders ordinarily welcome as collateral to guarantee the repayment of a loan. Since it is the easiest for banks to dispose of if the borrower is in default, a personal residence is the most acceptable real estate collateral. Many commercial buildings, with dependable leasing histories, are likewise satisfactory to secure debt. Land by itself, however, is customarily not accepted as collateral unless it is tacked on as additional security, or unless the land is part of a development project that demonstrates a consistent track record of tract sales.

If a business operates out of real estate it owns, the corporation's bank will usually permit the company to use the property as collateral to borrow money. When the business is the only tenant, though, the bank may restrict lending. How difficult will it be to sell the property if the business operation fails? The terms and conditions of a loan will be contingent on the answer to this question.

On the other hand, if the building in which the business operates is owned by the seller, the seller may prefer to keep the real estate and lease the property back to the buyer. If the building is free and clear, the rental income provides a monthly salary to the seller. In the event the business fails, and the seller is yet owed money, the seller takes back the business and continues to operate the company from the same location. Sometimes, tax implications determine whether a seller holds on to corporate real estate, or decides to sell it to the buyer.

Normal lending ratios vary, but 70% times the appraised value of the real estate is ordinarily what a conservative lender will advance to a borrower. 80% times the appraisal, or more, is not out of the question. Borrowing provisions are dependent more on the strength of the mortgagor than on the property. Most real estate closings require personal guarantees by the owner besides real estate collateral.

There are special lenders who will consider a loan application without the need of personal signatures, but the arrangement is usually costly and requires the borrower to put up substantial front money. A lender will always ask for as much collateral as it can get, and if the negotiator is desperate, or a novice, the bank continues to ask and ask and ask. Negotiation is the key, nonetheless.

Never think that a bank will not bargain, just because it asks for something out of the question.

Sharp buyers, when faced with a purchase that involves real estate, can sometimes add to the property appraisal by increasing lease revenues. Perhaps the space is only partly rented; new tenants will bring in more income. If the business to be purchased leases the building, raising the level of rent may also increase the appraised value. More value brings more money to the closing table, money often overlooked by less than keen buyers.

In the section describing notes - Chapter Twenty-One - a real estate note is one of the most common. This type of note is not only a secure investment, but offers the investor a higher than average return. Interest paid on a real estate note is usually higher than what is offered by most other forms of debt. When a real estate note is created as part of a business purchase, dependent on the credit of the debtor, there is a good chance that the note can be sold. Additional money is thereby brought to the closing table.

Buy That Business ... Poor old Daddy didn't Leave you!

Richard C. Shumaker, the author

In the mid-sixties, Richard graduated from West Virginia University with a Liberal Arts degree. After working for several large corporations, he decided to try self-employment; first, in real estate brokerage, then as a general contractor. Few can cite a greater number of real estate listings in 90 days: 53. And, not many can top his new home sales percentage over a 90-day period: 18 contracts from 25 contacts, or a 72% success ratio. But, when interest rates rose from 9% to 21% in the late 70's - curtailing construction starts - Richard turned aside from the building industry and dived into a succession of stimulating business ventures.

For example, in the early eighties, he packaged a limited partnership that purchased a prestigious nightclub ... the last of its kind between Las Vegas and Atlantic City. With over 150,000 square feet, the facility housed a 200 room motel, comedy club, numerous bars, restaurants and banquet halls, and a main dining room that served about 1,000 people. The comedy club hosted many stars such as Jay Leno, Jerry Seinfeld and Dennis Miller.

Later, another partnership was formed to acquire a 50 year old, well-known manufacturer of quality drapery products. Out of this operation came a window installation endeavor, commercial cabinet manufacturer and others. One operation made the top 100 list of the fastest growing US companies.

In 1987, Richard founded Hamilton Development Company to provide business clients with consultation expertise in areas of creative finance about corporate mergers and acquisitions. He developed an extensive portfolio of financing products able to efficiently and frugally leverage internal corporate strengths generally untapped by traditional financing methodology. These products enhance equity participation, reduce seller financing and provide greater levels of operational liquidity.

Shumaker is the originator of the Natural Business Philosophy; Syndicated Profit Reversal; the renowned AB Scenario; the Virtual Corporation; Controlled Daily Balance; Collateral Banking; and, the Gold Standard Security Enhancement Strategy. He founded WITT (Wilmerding Internet Think Tank), a group made up primarily of retired engineers from various Westinghouse companies whose function it is to perpetuate George Westinghouse's creative thinking for the benefit of the community.

In cooperation with the world famous Marx Trains Company, he designed, produced and marketed a limited collector's edition of an 1890 tinplate railroad boxcar inscribed 'Westinghouse Inter-Works Railway Co.' The railway was owned in the early 1900's by George Westinghouse.

Over the years, he has written how-to construction manuals, in-depth documentation designed to evaluate investment properties, financial enhancement guidelines, private placement proposals, newspaper articles and ... developed many timesaving, strength-improvement devices for new construction. Richard has also taught classes on real estate, financial matters and the Internet.

www.ingramcontent.com/pod-product-compliance
Lightning Source LLC
Chambersburg PA
CBHW051920170526
45168CB00001B/479